IMAGES
of America

FILIPINOS IN THE SAN FERNANDO VALLEY

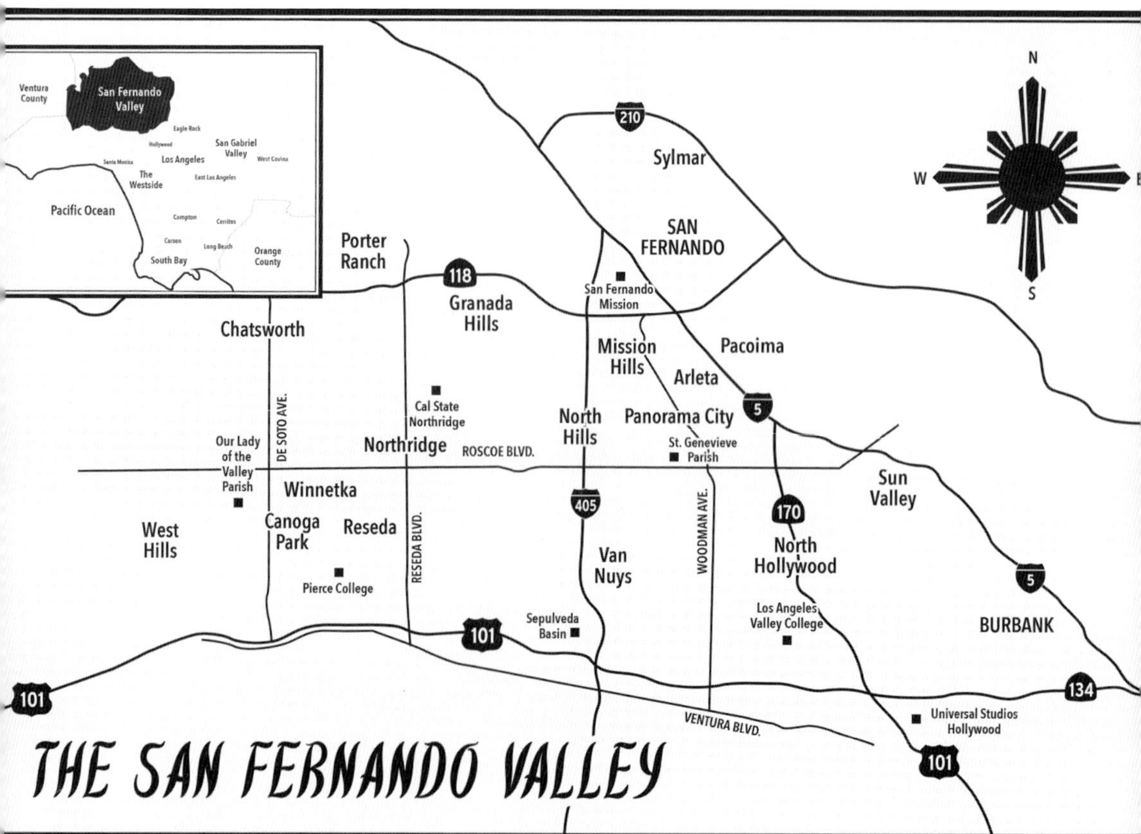

This map of the San Fernando Valley highlights certain neighborhoods and area landmarks and their location in relation to the broader Los Angeles Metropolitan Area. (Courtesy of Vincent Collyer.)

ON THE COVER: Family members and friends gather to celebrate the christening of Rosalinda Lee Escalona in the San Fernando Valley on July 5, 1947. (Courtesy of Shades of L.A. Photo Collection, Los Angeles Public Library.)

IMAGES
of America

FILIPINOS IN THE SAN FERNANDO VALLEY

Joseph Bernardo

ISBN 978-1-4671-6220-3

Published by Arcadia Publishing
Charleston, South Carolina

Printed in the United States of America

Library of Congress Control Number: 2025930363

For all general information, please contact Arcadia Publishing:
Telephone 843-853-2070
Fax 843-853-0044
E-mail sales@arcadiapublishing.com

Visit us on the Internet at www.arcadiapublishing.com

This book is dedicated to my favorite Valley Girl, Crisette Ligaya. Daddy loves you forever and ever.

Contents

Acknowledgments		6
Introduction		7
1.	Filipinos in the Agricultural and Industrial Valley	9
2.	Browning America's Suburb	21
3.	Filipino American Youth Culture	49
4.	Making Space and Place in the Valley	71
5.	Faces and Stories from Filipino American Suburbia	101
Bibliography		127

Acknowledgments

Though the cover bears my name, this book has undoubtedly been a collective effort. My deepest gratitude goes to the people who have gone out of their way in big and small ways to bring this project into reality. First and foremost, I thank those who shared their stories and photographs from their experiences in and with the San Fernando Valley: Gina Lopez Alexander; Erwin Altamira; Allan Aquino; Kathy Araneta-Delfin; Jomari Arciaga; Janel Barlongo; C.J. Berina; Adrienne Borlongan and J.P. Lopez of Wanderlust Creamery; Ralph Wilson Buado; Tracy Buenavista; Kristine Calara; Andrew Celi; Vincent Collyer; Jhenine Cordero; the late Antonio Cruz; Virgie Cruz; Alisa Damaso; Rachel DeGuzman; Anna Lisa De Guzman of Malaya Filipino American Dance Arts; Balagtas de la Cruz; Kristine de la Cruz; Lakandiwa de Leon; Elaine Dolalas; Rayson Esquejo; Marie Estrada; Reanne Estrada; Florante Ibanez; the Inez family; Jay-R; Moonie Lantion; Mina Layba; Arian and Dianne Leviste; Addison Magno, also known as Pare Young; Mike Makabenta; Gerardo Maravilla; Linda Marquez; Los Angeles city controller Kenneth Mejia; John Mina; Nate Mina; Lorenzo Mutia and other members of Anakbayan San Fernando Valley; the late Casimiro C. Obra; Cecile and Dante Ochoa; Christine Oriel of *Asian Journal*; Josefina Palma; Pamana Kali–San Fernando Valley; Aileen Domingo Paras; the Pilipino Workers Center; Berto Ponce; Randy Ramirez; Ray Ramirez; Max Reyes; the Roque family; Liza Makabenta Sacilioc; Christian Santiago; Janel Santos Kalaw; Arlyn Sinsay; Mara Shinn Smith; David Soriano; Elizabeth Soriano; Eduardo Soriano-Hewitt; Susan Suh; Elnora Tayag; Nenette Tenza-Umali; Char Vega; Vanessa Vela-Lovelace; Butch "Tracer One" Velez; Melissa Veluz; Madison Villanueva; and Carl Angelo Viray. My sincere apologies to anyone whom I forgot to acknowledge.

I am also indebted to the librarians and archivists at the various institutions where I found photographs for this book. Thank you to the caretakers of the Associated Press, the Filipinos in Ventura County Digital Photo Collection at CSU–Channel Islands, the *Los Angeles Times* Photo Collection at UCLA, the San Fernando Valley Digital History Library at CSUN, and Shades of L.A. Collection at the Los Angeles Public Library. Thank you to Caroline Vickerson of Arcadia Publishing for keeping my progress on this project from going by the wayside.

Finally, thank you to my many colleagues and friends who lent their love, support, and laughter throughout my life. Thank you to my nuclear and extended family whose legacies began in the Valley. To Carmencita and Luis Bernardo and my late *lola* Telesfora Bernardo, thank you for instilling in me the idea of "home" so that I know where my passions should lie. To my Gerlie, you are my everything (sometimes). Thank you for always pushing me beyond my imaginary limits. *Mahal kita* forever and ever. Lastly, to my Crissy girl, I cannot wait for you to become an advocate and caretaker of all that is good. Thank you for making everything worth it.

Introduction

I'm gonna settle down and never more roam. And make the San Fernando Valley my home.

—"San Fernando Valley," Bing Crosby, 1944

Today, over 1.8 million people followed what Bing Crosby crooned in his 1944 hit song and made the San Fernando Valley their home. If this 260-square-mile area were a single city, it would be the fifth largest in the United States. Yet, before suburbanites descended upon "the Valley" to "never more roam," it has been home to countless people throughout the centuries. The Tongva, Tataviam, and Chumash peoples were among the first known caretakers of the Valley, inhabiting its foothills. In 1797, Spanish missionaries built the Mission San Fernando Rey de España at the site of the Indigenous village Achooykomenga to centralize colonization efforts. When Mexico gained independence from Spain in 1821, Californios wrested the lands of the Valley from the church and divided them into ranchos. After the Americans colonized California following the Mexican-American War in 1848, white settlers built an infrastructure of railroads, boom towns, agricultural fields, and livestock farms that dominated the landscape for decades. By the early 20th century, a few white developers controlled the land, facilitating development and the eventual annexation of most of the Valley into the city of Los Angeles after the construction of the Los Angeles Aqueduct in 1915. The burgeoning movie industry gained a foothold in the Valley beginning in the 1910s, finding ample room for large studio lots. Entertainment companies like Universal, Warner Bros., and Disney established their corporate headquarters in the area. After World War II, the San Fernando Valley experienced significant growth, spearheading the nation's suburban development through Keynesian, state-directed economic policies. The construction of new suburban developments, freeways, shopping centers, and schools attracted many families, transforming the Valley into a symbol of postwar American abundance. Despite its wealth, the Valley has also been a target of criticism with its uncontrolled suburban sprawl, cultural plainness, and unbearable heat during summers, even amongst its residents. It has been deemed the capital of nowhere, a nest for white American heteronormativity, and the epicenter of pornography. For many, the San Fernando Valley has been a symbol of suburban decay since the 1970s. Yet, for all its multiple forms and identities, it continues to be a place of aspiration for many communities of color.

This is where the story of this book begins. The San Fernando Valley happens to be my home. My parents spent their first three years in the United States in an apartment building with other newly immigrated Filipino families just outside of what is now known as Historic Filipinotown in central Los Angeles. By the late 1970s, most of those families purchased homes in the Valley, becoming among the first Filipinos in their neighborhoods. My parents migrated to the Valley after purchasing a newly built three-bedroom home in Northridge for $68,000 in 1976. Thousands of Filipinos followed a similar pattern and migrated to the Valley over the next few decades. By 2020, a total of 78,477 Filipinos made the San Fernando Valley their home.

Like photographs themselves, this book provides a momentary glimpse of some experiences of Valley Filipinos. It begins with a brief look at the handful of Filipinos who lived and worked here prior to the 1960s, referred to by Asian American historians as the "Manong generation," and their offspring, the "Bridge generation." However, much of the book is devoted to the generation who came to the Valley after the 1965 Immigration Act, the key legislation that dramatically changed the demographic makeup of the United States. Many of the photographs in the following pages reflect how Filipinos helped reshape the place author Kevin Roderick calls "America's Suburb," particularly during the 1970s, 1980s, and 1990s, when a restructuring global economy brought dramatic changes to metropolitan landscapes.

One cannot tell this local history without underscoring the larger context of Southern California's connection to the world and the history of racism. Through understanding the history of the US empire in the Philippines and elsewhere in the world as well as the fight for civil rights in housing, one can make sense of the evolving landscape of Los Angeles. Through entertainment magic, the San Fernando Valley has been a stand-in for "Anytown, U.S.A." in countless movies and television shows. As these images are projected nationally and globally, they create cultural desires of living for communities of color. After decades of immigration and desegregation, these historically marginalized groups have remade the cities and neighborhoods of Southern California. They diversified the suburbs racially and economically and intentionally (and unintentionally) challenged the traditional boundaries of (sub)urbanity, heteronormativity, and whiteness, much to the chagrin of some of their older, whiter neighbors. This book is a glimpse of this period of dramatic demographic and cultural changes in suburbia through the camera lenses of a handful of Filipino families.

Documenting the history of Filipinos in the San Fernando Valley did have challenges. The City of Los Angeles has structured much of the Valley politically to limit civic participation. There are very few Filipino organizations representing the region or public festivals that gather the community together. Filipino Americans, with their colonial desire to acculturate, tend to blend into the suburban landscape. So how does one find Filipinos in this culturally anonymous jungle of tract housing, strip malls, asphalt streets, and concrete freeways? Recalling Karen Tongson's *Relocations*, this book weaves through suburbia's "nowhere" spaces. Most of the photographs compiled in this book took place where most Filipinos in the Valley were—in their private homes and neighborhoods. They are what Filipino Americans cared about the most—family, community, spirituality, and play—and not necessarily their obligations to work or civic duty. They also tell diverse stories—some of embracing heteronormativity and consumerism, others of fighting for social justice. Most photographs, however, lie somewhere in between. In essence, telling a pictorial story of this community required making sense of the seemingly illegible suburban landscape, finding meaning in not-so-obvious places, and nuancing the Filipino American experience.

The history of Filipinos in the San Fernando Valley conveys a prototypical Filipino colonial settlement in the United States. Most Filipino Americans across the United States live in traditional car-centric, privatized suburban areas outside of central cities. In 2020, for example, approximately 85 percent of the more than 703,000 Filipinos in the five-county greater Los Angeles region lived in suburban communities. Life in the changing suburbs is what many Filipinos throughout the Global North experience. Filipino American history over the last 50 years, in many ways, is largely a suburban history. Yet little has been written about Filipinos in these particular spaces.

Finally, this is by no means an exhaustive history. No book can ever serve such a function. *Filipinos in the San Fernando Valley* covers only a fraction of the 80,000 Filipinos who call (or called) the Valley home. This history is ever evolving. As many Filipino families continue to move to the Valley and younger residents move for "greener pastures" in Santa Clarita, Palmdale, Ventura County, and even Las Vegas, the future of Filipinos in the Valley remains uncertain and deserves more documentation and study. I hope that this work of archiving and mapping this community through photography does spark interest in more popular and academic works on Filipino Americans, the San Fernando Valley, and suburbia in general.

One

Filipinos in the Agricultural and Industrial Valley

Los Angeles's San Fernando Valley decades prior to World War II was a sparsely populated agricultural hub. By the time the much of the region was annexed by the City of Los Angeles, its population was roughly 3,000 people. As the Southern Pacific rail line made its way to the San Fernando Valley and water irrigation became readily available by the early 20th century, small-scale agricultural farming exponentially increased across the Valley. The region was one of the largest wheat producers in the United States at the time. Citrus farms eventually lined areas like Encino, Canoga Park, Zelzah (now Northridge), and Pacoima. Dairy and poultry farms were abundant in North Hollywood, Arleta, Van Nuys, and Reseda. By the 1930s, agriculture in the Valley was at its height.

At the same time, Filipinos had migrated to the United States in unprecedented numbers as agribusiness on the West Coast began recruiting America's colonial subjects as cheap labor to work on their farms. Known as the "Manong Generation," these Filipinos who came largely from the provincial areas of the Philippines worked in the agricultural and service sectors during this era. Some Filipinos traveled seasonally to the San Fernando Valley as laborers to farms such as Sunshine Ranch in what became Granada Hills, picking citrus and other crops. A few settled and made homes in the area, particularly in the northeast Valley in San Fernando and Pacoima, where most people of color were segregated at the time. There, Filipinos built community with other ethnic and racial groups.

By the 1940s, the San Fernando Valley had become a primary target for Los Angeles city officials and developers who wanted to build suburban neighborhoods. By the 1960s, the Valley was one of the fastest-growing regions in the country. Panorama City, for example, was the Valley's first planned community and was an exemplar of suburban development in California. A handful of Filipinos were able to move to these neighborhoods and work in the region's industrial plants during this era, but this post–World War II prosperity was designed primarily for white, middle-class families. The small number of Filipino Americans who did make the Valley their home during these decades nonetheless built a community and culture for themselves, challenged conventional standards, and resisted marginalization in many ways. This chapter highlights some of the experiences of those few prior to the 1970s when the area transitioned from an agricultural center to a white suburban haven.

Before the post–World War II suburban boom, the San Fernando Valley was an agricultural center during the late 19th and early 20th centuries with large swaths of agricultural fields dominating much of the landscape. As an example of pre–World War II land use, here is an aerial view of the area known as Woodland Hills. (Courtesy of San Fernando Valley Digital History Library/Special Collections and Archives, University Library, California State University, Northridge.)

A group of Filipinos poses at a citrus farm in the early 1930s. For much of the first half of the 20th century, Filipino American history was largely agricultural. Most of the Filipino migrants who came to the United States during the 1920s worked as farmworkers. Many worked the farms in the San Fernando Valley, harvesting crops for distribution. (Courtesy of Shades of L.A. Photo Collection, Los Angeles Public Library.)

Filipinos who did settle in the San Fernando Valley lived mostly in the northeast sections of Pacoima, Sylmar, and the city of San Fernando. Tom (left, last name unknown) stands beside his friend in front of his brand-new car at his Valley home in 1939. (Courtesy of Shades of L.A. Photo Collection, Los Angeles Public Library.)

Though Filipino men comprised the vast majority of migrants from the Philippines, a handful of Filipina women also came to the United States. Amalia Ines is pictured here posing in front of a car in San Fernando during the 1930s. She worked with her spouse, Marcelino Ines Sr., as labor contractors in the San Fernando Valley, helping to get other Filipinos farm laborer jobs. (Courtesy of Florante Ibanez.)

A popular social outlet among Filipinos during the 1940s was large ballroom galas. Usually hosted by an organization, these gatherings included a big band and ballroom dancing for hours. Many historical pictures of Filipino Americans are of large group shots at galas. They reveal the era's sexual politics. Given the community's demographics of the time, where men outnumbered women 14:1, and the anti-miscegenation legislation, which prohibited and discouraged Filipinos

from cohabiting outside of their race, many of these interracial couples pictured are defying oppressive laws and cultures. Seen here is the gala of the San Fernando Valley Women's Club on February 1, 1941. Among the attendees are Dalmacio Soriano (middle row standing, third from left), Emilia Soriano (seated third from right), and Trinidad Ventura (seated fourth from right). (Courtesy of California State University, Channel Islands, John Spoor Broome Library.)

When they were not working, Filipinos gathered for social and recreational activities. In the image at left, a few friends meet for a game of tennis in an unidentified park in the Valley. Below are two friends, identified only as Pat (left) and Tom (right), at a gathering outside of a home in the San Fernando Valley during the late 1930s. (Both, courtesy of Shades of L.A. Photo Collection, Los Angeles Public Library.)

Organizations, especially Masonic fraternities, were vital to maintain sociality among Filipino Americans. Though most, if not all, Filipino American organizations were based in the central Los Angeles area, some found community in the Valley. Seen here is a Pinoy in 1947 who became involved in a mainstream Masonic lodge and even became the grand master of North Hollywood's Eureka Masonic Lodge. (Courtesy of Shades of L.A. Photo Collection, Los Angeles Public Library.)

As part of the imperial policy in the Philippines, the United States built military bases in the Philippines while also allowing Filipinos to enlist in the US Navy. For most Filipinos, joining the US Navy was an avenue to immigrate. Pictured here are sisters Gloria (left) and Dolores Ilejay (right) posing with their friend Amado during his visit to the Valley in 1952. (Courtesy of Shades of L.A. Photo Collection, Los Angeles Public Library.)

Like many Americans, Filipino Americans experienced a small "baby boom" after World War II, transforming the large bachelor community. Legislation like the War Brides Act of 1945 and the abolishment of anti-miscegenation laws in California in 1948 allowed more Filipino men to marry and raise families. This is a photograph of a baby christening in Pacoima in 1950. Gloria Ilejay Balucas is standing second from the left. Standing fourth from left is Dolores Ilejay Arlington, godmother to the unidentified child. Below is Mabel Ilejay's family celebrating a birthday party in 1950 at the Ilejay home on Desmond Street in Pacoima. Included in the image is Gloria Balucas on the back row, far left. Gloria's mother, Mabel Ilejay, is fifth from left. Dolores Ilejay is seventh from left. (Both, courtesy of Shades of L.A. Photo Collection, Los Angeles Public Library; above, photograph by Casimiro C. Obra.)

A handful of Filipino Americans attended San Fernando High School throughout its history. Pictured is a young couple at their prom at San Fernando High School in 1953. (Courtesy of Shades of L.A. Photo Collection, Los Angeles Public Library/White's Studios.)

Here is Sam Balucas doing the popular limbo at a birthday party at his aunt's Lake View Terrace house in 1962. Balucas moved to the Valley in 1961 and worked for Hughes Aircraft Company until he retired in 1989. He was a long-time leader of the Filipino American National Historical Society Los Angeles Chapter until he passed in 2007. (Courtesy of Shades of L.A. Photo Collection, Los Angeles Public Library.)

Suburban bowling alleys began sprouting across the United States as the sport's popularity skyrocketed during the post–World War II era. Pictured are bowling league participants in 1963 at the Ronnell Bowling Alley, located at 12385 San Fernando Road in Sylmar. From left to right are (kneeling) Gloria Balucas and Frances Pilar; (standing) Sam Balucas and Fred Lomboy. (Courtesy of Shades of L.A. Photo Collection, Los Angeles Public Library.)

Here are three men eating dinner at a restaurant in San Fernando. From left to right are unidentified, John Ilejay, and Robert Ilejay. (Courtesy of Shades of L.A. Photo Collection, Los Angeles Public Library and Casimiro C. Obra.)

Carlos Romulo (center), the longtime Philippine ambassador and founding member of the United Nations, attends the Executives' Dinner Club of Van Nuys banquet in 1961 to promote Philippine–US relations as part of Cold War imperial policy. With Romulo are, from left to right, Bill Ridgeway, general manager of the Panorama Shopping Center, Mrs. Ridgeway, Mrs. Pine, and Frank W. Pine of the San Fernando Valley Industrial Association. (Courtesy of Valley Times Collection, Los Angeles Public Library.)

Filipino community leaders gather at Joseph Batugo's Chatsworth home in 1964 to honor Earl Carroll, founder of Philippine American Life and General Insurance Company. Pictured from left to right are Benjamin Manibog, president, Filipino American Community of Los Angeles (FACLA); Monty Manibog; Bernadine Batugo; Darlena Batugo Herrick, 1961 Miss Philippines of Los Angeles; and Ramon Barretto, Los Angeles general manager of Philippine Airlines. (Courtesy of Shades of L.A. Photo Collection, Los Angeles Public Library.)

Darlena Batugo served as Miss Philippines of Los Angeles in 1961. As a second-generation Filipino American, Batugo had not visited the Philippines but aspired to visit her father's homeland one day according to local newspaper *Valley Times* on July 15, 1961. (Courtesy of Shades of L.A. Photo Collection, Los Angeles Public Library.)

The Ro-Shons was an amateur band formed by the Ines and Suetos families during the early 1960s. They played in venues throughout the San Fernando Valley and beyond. Pictured from left to right are Jim Inez, unidentified, Benjamita Ines, Gladys Ines-Jenkins, unidentified, Marcel Suetos, Matias Ines Jr., Floren Suetos, and Matias Ines Sr. (Courtesy of Florante Ibanez.)

Two

Browning America's Suburb

As a result of the 1965 Hart-Cellar Act (or 1965 Immigration Act), which expanded quotas to facilitate more immigrants to work in the United States and reunite with families, the Filipino American population expanded dramatically. From 1960 to 1980, the Filipino community in the United States grew by 339.37 percent. Unlike prior immigration waves, post-1965 immigrants included many women and families, and most worked in the service sector or as white-collar professionals, reflecting a post-industrial American economy. Southern California was the largest recipient of these new immigrants. Hundreds of thousands of Filipinos came to Los Angeles because of the 1965 Immigration Act, with many starting in the central Los Angeles/Historic Filipinotown area. Facilitated by African American organizing during the civil rights movement and the passage of the Fair Housing Act in 1968, many Filipinos were able to move to formerly segregated suburban areas by the 1970s and 1980s. Most in Southern California found homes in areas like Carson, Cerritos, West Covina, and Eagle Rock and in the neighborhoods of the San Fernando Valley.

In 1960, approximately 92 percent of the Valley was white, and most were middle class. In subsequent decades, the region attracted many communities of color from all economic classes who sought affordable housing. By 1990, there were 26,927 Filipinos in the Valley. Many settled across the Valley, where they purchased homes in older subdivisions or in newly built communities. Others rented apartments in more densely populated areas. Working- and middle-class neighborhoods like Panorama City, Arleta, and North Hollywood in the eastern part of the Valley and Canoga Park, Winnetka, and Reseda in the western part became concentrated sites of Filipinos as many whites began leaving those areas. Panorama City emerged as the epicenter for Filipino Americans in the Valley by the 1980s.

Like many areas across the United States, the San Fernando Valley was a place where many Filipinos lived out their versions of the American Dream they consumed through popular culture in the Philippines. They aimed to attain a suburban home, a two-car garage, and a neighborhood to raise kids for college—the archetypal life of middle-class abundance. As they joined many communities of color to diversify the Valley, whites bemoaned the urban "deterioration" of suburbia as the Valley became less white and middle class. This chapter looks at some of the pioneering Filipino American families that helped "brown" the San Fernando Valley during a time of cultural and demographic transition.

Panorama City, developed by Fritz B. Burns and Henry Kaiser in the late 1940s, was the Valley's first planned community and an exemplar of suburban development in California. At the time, racial housing covenants declared that no Panorama City lot would be "used or occupied by any person whose blood is not entirely that of the white or Caucasian race," creating white generational wealth. By the 1970s, whites fled Panorama City as the area became more integrated with many immigrants, including many Filipinos. By the 1980s, Panorama City had the highest concentration of Filipinos in the Valley, quickly becoming a community epicenter. Pictured here is an aerial view of Panorama City in 1950. Below is a street-level view of newly built Panorama City. (Above, courtesy of Shades of L.A. Photo Collection, Los Angeles Public Library; below, courtesy Los Angeles Times Photo Collection/UCLA.)

As more Filipinos moved into homes in the San Fernando Valley, homeownership became a sense of pride and economic attainment. Many families took photographs in front of their homes as a rite of passage into American life. Leni Barretto Shinn and her two children, Mara and John J., stand in front of their family home in Panorama City during the early 1980s. Below are Proni Ramirez and her daughter Remy standing in front of their Panorama City home in 1976. (Above, courtesy of Mara Shinn Smith; below, courtesy of Ray Ramirez.)

Originally incorporated as the town of Marian in 1912, the Reseda neighborhood of Los Angeles became one of the premier areas to live after World War II. By the 1970s and 1980s, families of color began moving into the neighborhood, seeing it as a symbol of upward mobility. Here is the Domingo family in front of their newly purchased Reseda home during the late 1970s. (Courtesy of Aileen Domingo Paras.)

Angelita Leviste and her children Jessica and Arian are in front of their brand-new Canoga Park home and car in 1981. Canoga Park, originally called Owensmouth, was founded in 1912 and annexed to the city of Los Angeles in 1917. Suburban housing development in the area continued well into the 1980s as developers sought to build homes on former agricultural lands. (Courtesy of the Leviste family.)

Van Nuys was founded in 1911 and annexed to the city of Los Angeles in 1915. The neighborhood of apartments and single-family houses also became the Valley's government civic center. By the 1970s and 1980s, Van Nuys's demographics shifted, bringing much class, racial, and linguistic diversity. Exemplifying this shift are the Veluz children, who stand in front of their family home in Van Nuys in 1982. (Courtesy of Melissa Veluz.)

Chatsworth became part of the city of Los Angeles in 1915. When post–World War II development came to the Valley, many locals resisted encroaching suburban homes. Remnants of the "Old West" such as horse trails, ranches, and stagecoach motifs can still be found throughout the neighborhood. Houses nonetheless did get built, purchased by a diversity of families. The Makabenta family is pictured at their Chatsworth home during the 1970s. (Courtesy of Mike Makabenta.)

Winnetka was founded in 1922 as a small farming community known as the Weeks Poultry Colony. After the defeat of discriminatory housing covenants, Winnetka became one of the most ethnically diverse neighborhoods in the San Fernando Valley. Seen here is the Layba family in front of their Winnetka home in 1979. (Courtesy of Mina Layba.)

North Hollywood has seen many changes since its formal incorporation into the city of Los Angeles in 1923. The northern section of North Hollywood has been a destination for immigrants since the 1970s. Recently, the neighborhood's southern end experienced an economic resurgence. Pictured from left to right are Neny Sawit, Rayson Esquejo, Earl Valencia, Aileen Valencia, Erwin Valencia, and Sheryl Beran at their North Hollywood home during the 1980s. (Courtesy of Rayson Esquejo.)

As space to build large-scale housing developments became rarer by the 1980s, developers began building more townhomes and apartment complexes across the Valley to accommodate the growing housing demand. Pictured at right are Elvessa Dolalas and her daughter Elaine in front of their Sepulveda (now North Hills) townhome in the early 1980s. Below are Randy Ramirez Sr. and Randy Jr. posing in front of their Sepulveda apartment and their blue family van in 1981. Sepulveda rebranded its name to North Hills in 1991. (Right, courtesy of Elaine Dolalas; below, courtesy of the Ramirez family.)

By the 1990s, thousands of Filipinos had moved to the San Fernando Valley. Many continue to purchase and rent homes, further diversifying the region. Seen here is a gathering of two generations of cousins in front of the home of the Damaso family in Reseda in 1994. (Courtesy of Alisa Damaso.)

Often in immigrant communities, one household plays the part of "Ellis Island" for the entire extended family where newly arrived immigrants stay until they are financially stable enough to find a place of their own. Pictured are the Altamira brothers at their grandfather's apartment in Panorama City welcoming their newly immigrated cousins from Quezon, Philippines, during the 1990s. (Courtesy of Erwin Altamira.)

As many Filipinos immigrated to the United States during the 1960s and 1970s, many threw informal house parties to celebrate all kinds of occasions. Above is a group of Pinoys at a party in the backyard of Carlos Sinsay's Canoga Park home during the late 1970s. The lone child in the photograph is Aileen Domingo Paras with her father, Archimedes Domingo. At right are Antonio and Virgie Cruz dancing on their backyard patio in Canoga Park at a party in the same era. (Above, courtesy of the Leviste family; right, courtesy of the Cruz family.)

During the American colonial period in the Philippines, Americans introduced basketball as part of their pacifying efforts. Basketball continues to be the most popular sport among Filipinos. *Lusot*, which translates to "pass-through" in Cebuano and Tagalog, is a tradition where the losing team must crawl underneath the legs of the winners. Luis Bernardo crawls under the winners of a backyard basketball game in 1985. (Courtesy of Aileen Domingo Paras.)

As social gatherings became larger, more elaborate and organized set-ups were necessary. Pictured here is Archimedes Domingo MCing a party underneath a tent set up on the backyard patio during the mid-1980s. (Courtesy of Aileen Domingo Paras.)

Family gatherings are a ubiquitous experience among many Filipino Americans. Houses become filled with extended family and friends. Seen here is the Gamalinda family reunion at the Aquino North Hills home in 1983. Below, Linda Marquez receives a gift from her cousin, Archimedes Domingo, who is dressed up in a makeshift Santa Claus costume during a family Christmas party in Northridge in 1984. (Above, courtesy of Allan Aquino; below, courtesy of Linda Marquez.)

Food is central at most gatherings. The Ramirez family and their recent addition, Randy Jr., are pictured grilling Filipino barbecue at their family home in Reseda in 1981. Pictured below is perhaps one of the most familiar poses at a Filipino American gathering, a group gathered with the food buffet table as the centerpiece. (Above, courtesy of the Ramirez family; below, courtesy of Aileen Domingo Paras.)

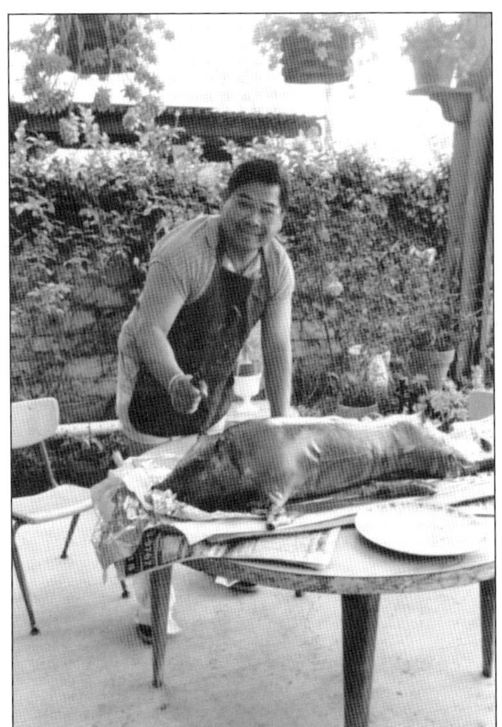

As a centerpiece to many very special Filipino gatherings, the *lechon* pig gathers the most attention. Sulo Layba prepares to cut the lechon pig in the backyard of their Winnetka home for a family celebration, while small children (below) take a peek at the lechon at a birthday party in 1978. (Right, courtesy of Mina Layba; below, courtesy of Mara Shinn Smith.)

As immigrants settled in the United States and gained citizenship, many took the opportunity to petition other family members and other loved ones to join them, creating larger, multigenerational households. This "chain migration" allowed extended families to form among many immigrants, including Filipino Americans. Here are the patriarch and matriarch of the Descallar clan in the United States, Gabino and Isabel Descallar, dancing and singing karaoke as they celebrate their 50th wedding anniversary with their children, grandchildren, and others. (Both, courtesy of Elaine Dolalas.)

Karaoke is a modern Philippine pastime and a staple at many gatherings since its invention in the 1970s. In Filipino American households across the United States, living rooms are transformed into stages where many generations hone their singing skills and perform their favorite tunes. Angelito Leviste is pictured singing on an early karaoke machine, known among Filipinos then as "minus-one," at a New Year's party in Arleta. (Courtesy of the Leviste family.)

As karaoke gained extreme popularity among Filipino men, many early adopters emulated the American and Filipino crooners they grew up with. As an example, here are the Shinn family men belting out a karaoke tune during a family gathering in Panorama City. (Courtesy of Mara Shinn Smith.)

A karaoke session can occur during a special occasion or at a random time of day. Those who participated can attest that karaoke builds community through shedding inhibitions and exuding joy. Pictured above are, from left to right, Archimedes Domingo, Jimmy Leviste, Luis Bernardo, and Ruel Torres singing their hearts out in karaoke at a party during the late 1980s. Below are Dion Torres (holding the mic) and friends enjoying a casual night of karaoke at the home of Bal and Celia de la Cruz in Panorama City. (Above, courtesy of Aileen Domingo Paras; below, courtesy of the de la Cruz family.)

As karaoke technology advanced, Filipino families bought the latest machines for their living rooms. Seen here is a karaoke session using the "Magic Mic," which was very popular during the early 2000s, at the Ochoa household in North Hollywood. (Courtesy of the Ochoa family.)

Mahjong is a tile-based game developed in China that gained wide popularity in the Philippines and elsewhere in the world. A game that is played in many Filipino American living rooms, backyards, and basements, mahjong allows players to socialize, gossip, and gamble at the same time. The Layba family plays mahjong in the living room of their Winnetka home during a family gathering. (Courtesy of Mina Layba.)

Given the Valley's terrain and relatively open roads, many cyclists spend weekends riding across the region. This group of Pinoys in matching uniforms poses for a picture in front of the Canoga Park home of Angelito Leviste in 1978 after a long ride around the San Fernando Valley. Typically, after a long morning ride, the group of cyclists gathered at someone's home to eat a Filipino breakfast, defeating the purpose of the exercise as some joked. This tradition lasted for many years. Pictured from left to right are Angelito Reyes Sr., Antonio Cruz, Luis Bernardo, Archimedes Domingo, Rico Reyes, Fidel Reyes, Jaime Leviste, and Angelito Leviste. (Courtesy of the Bernardo family.)

Filipinos made their homes in both private and public spaces across the Valley. Seen here from left to right are Honorata Carlos, Ermelinda Sinsay, Lucita Carlos, Christine Sinsay Torres, Arlyn Sinsay, and Lorenz Carlos in the backyard of their Northridge home during the early 1980s. Below, Randy (left) and Ray Ramirez are up high in a tree at Woodley Park in 1980. (Above, courtesy of Arlyn Sinsay; below, courtesy of Ray Ramirez.)

In car-centric Southern California, particularly in suburbia, vehicles are an absolute necessity as well as a symbol of middle-class status. With many Filipinos having larger families than prototypical American nuclear families, larger vans were especially popular among Filipino Americans in the San Fernando Valley who sought to transport families around the area, go on road trips around California and beyond, and engage in recreational activities like camping and fishing. Tagumpay de Leon is in front of his newly purchased Chevy Astro Van with his four-year-old daughter Hiyas inside at their home in Burbank in 1986. Below is Fr. Frank Makabenta with his niece Liza in front of a brand-new RV at the Makabenta home in Chatsworth (Left, courtesy of Lakandiwa de Leon; below, courtesy of Liza Makabenta Sacilioc.)

Posing for a photograph in front of a vehicle, as scholars have argued, can convey aspiration for economic and social achievement in the United States. Here is Balagtas "Boyong" de la Cruz posing in front of his newly purchased Dodge Ram van at his Panorama City home during the early 1980s. (Courtesy of the de la Cruz family.)

The Ramirez family owned many vehicles upon arrival in the San Fernando Valley. This is a view of Peter Ramirez from inside the Ramirez family van in Reseda during the early 1980s. (Courtesy of Ray Ramirez.)

Many post-1965 Filipino immigrants came to the United States with families, which differed from earlier migration waves of Filipinos. By the 1970s and 1980s, many young Filipino Americans were born and/or raised in American society. Seen here is young Michael Makabenta in his toy car in front of his house in Chatsworth, and below is Mara Shinn Smith on her bicycle next to St. Genevieve School in Panorama City during the 1970s. (Above, courtesy of Mike Makabenta; below, courtesy of Mara Shinn Smith.)

The San Fernando Valley can get notoriously hot during the summer with temperatures reaching triple digits. Many residents will find any way to cool off, as young Mara Shinn Smith and John Shinn do with a water hose on their driveway in Panorama City in the summer of 1978. (Courtesy of Mara Shinn Smith.)

Here are young second-generation Filipino American boys posing with their toy guns in front of a swimming pool under construction. This was taken at the Esteban residence in Sun Valley. (Courtesy of the Leviste family.)

Parlor games are a staple at many Filipino gatherings as they bring amusement for both adults and kids alike. Young boys enjoy a parlor game during a Christmas party in 1980. (Courtesy of Aileen Domingo Paras.)

Young girls jump for joy on a pedestrian bridge headed to Reseda Park during the early 1980s. The park was first built in 1931 and expanded during the 1960s as the area's population boomed. (Courtesy of Aileen Domingo Paras.)

As many Filipino immigrants come to the United States, they begin to adapt to some American cultural customs that were not practiced in the Philippines. Above is Thelma Buado preparing her daughter in their apartment for a Halloween parade at Lemay Street Elementary School in Lake Balboa (formerly part of Van Nuys) during the 1980s. Below are the Altamira, Torres, and Cabrera children getting ready for a night of trick-or-treating in Arleta in 1980. (Above, courtesy of Ralph Buado; below, courtesy of Erwin Altamira.)

The Boy Scout program was introduced to the Philippines in the early 20th century as a program of American colonization. As many Filipinos migrated to the United States, some young boys joined the Scouts as part of their extracurricular activities. At left is a young Nathaniel Mina doing a Boy Scout salute at the Burbank Elks Lodge, and below are Nathaniel with his fellow Boy Scouts Winston Ruiz (left) and Wilfred Ruiz (right). (Both, courtesy of Nathaniel V. Mina.)

Baseball little leagues are rites of passage for many Americans, influencing the childhoods of many young Valley residents. Seen here are young Judy Descallar (left) and Elaine Dolalas at a baseball dugout in a park in Tujunga. (Courtesy of Elaine Dolalas.)

Aprille Grace Buado stands in front of the family station wagon at a strip mall in Reseda during the 1980s. This stretch of Sherman Way at Reseda Boulevard lay at the heart of Reseda and exemplified post–World War II abundance for a time. (Courtesy of Ralph Wilson Buado.)

The St. Genevieve's School kindergarten class of 1986 conveys the demographic changes of the church and the neighborhood of the time. By this time, Filipino, Mexican, Salvadoran, and other immigrant communities began to comprise the majority of the church congregation and student population as post–World War II white families fled elsewhere. (Courtesy of Elaine Dolalas.)

The Tiongson-Reyes kids enjoy a day with friends at the newly opened Lake Balboa Park during the early 1990s. The park is part of the Sepulveda Basin, the largest public open space in the San Fernando Valley, spanning more than 2,000 acres. (Courtesy of Max Reyes.)

Three

Filipino American Youth Culture

As many historians and sociologists have noted, the "teenager" emerged as a distinct demographic in post–World War II American suburbia. The confluence of expanding education, growing economy, and geographic dispersion due to the automobile created a unique culture that differed from childhood and adulthood. The entertainment industry began observing the San Fernando Valley for its emergence of youth culture as an exemplar for the nation. From cruising Van Nuys Boulevard to "Valley Girl" mall rats at the Sherman Oaks Galleria to the karate dojos of Reseda to the dystopian gang-infested public high schools by the 1990s, Hollywood looked to the Valley as a forefront of teenage popular culture.

Second-generation Filipino Americans born and raised in the United States also created a unique youth culture of their own as they came of age in the 1980s and 1990s. Along with other Filipino youths in California, Filipino kids in the Valley had their own slang, fashion, and ways of being. It reflected their cultural heritage, suburban upbringing, and multi-ethnic environments. It was influenced by American popular cultural forms like hip hop and the exchanges between white, Black, Latino, and other Asian youths. It could be mapped geographically and cognitively.

Many expressions of Filipino youth emerged during this period. Immersed in Southern California car culture, Filipino American youths invested in altering Japanese imported cars to reflect a particular Asian American experience. As street gangs exponentially grew across Los Angeles, Filipino American gangs such as Real Pinoy Brothers (RPB), Jefrox (JFX), and others found bases in the Valley as protection, even garnering notoriety in the mainstream press. Dance crews, party crews, racing crews, and other types of groups formed and varied according to interests, class, and geographic proximity to other Filipino Americans.

The area's institutions of higher education were also sites of Filipino American youth culture. At a time when many communities of color entered colleges and universities in higher numbers, a group of Filipinos at California State University at Northridge (CSUN) founded the Filipino American Student Association (FASA), an influential organization that became one of the few youth voices in the sprawling San Fernando Valley. Filipino student clubs at other schools emerged as well. The photographs in this chapter convey some of this emerging culture of Filipino American youth during the 1980s and 1990s, which the author suggests both embraced and defied American cultural forces during this pivotal time in history.

Roma Mina, who immigrated to the United States in 1978, immediately acclimated to American society. Here, she poses for her team volleyball pictures for St. Finbar School in Burbank during the mid-1980s. (Courtesy of Nathaniel V. Mina.)

Reanne Estrada, who grew up in the San Fernando Valley, is a public visual artist and cofounder of Public Matters, a creative studio for civic engagement based in Los Angeles. She is pictured during her Reseda High School cheerleading days in the mid-1980s. (Courtesy of Marie and Reanne Estrada.)

In classic Americana fashion, here is Ray Ramirez sitting atop his beloved 1980 Chevy Camaro. This picture was taken in front of their Reseda home. (Courtesy of Ray Ramirez.)

During the 1980s, scooters gained popularity in the United States, with Japanese manufacturers like Honda penetrating the American market. Here, young Nenette Tenza-Umali poses in front of a Honda Elite scooter in Panorama City during the late 1980s. (Courtesy of Nenette Tenza-Umali.)

St. Genevieve High School in Panorama City opened its doors to the growing population in the San Fernando Valley in the 1950s. By the 1980s, St. Genevieve's parish and school had the largest concentration of Filipinos in the Valley despite an overall enrollment decline since the 1970s. This section of the school was known colloquially as "Flip Alley" among some students. Here are young Pinays (and one man) posing at Flip Alley during the late 1980s. Below is a group of young Filipina teenagers at St. Genevieve School in 1989. (Both, courtesy of Aileen Domingo Paras.)

By the late 1980s, many young Filipino Americans in the Valley adopted a distinct look and fashion sense influenced by American popular culture and other communities of color in Southern California. Allan Aquino (far left) is with his cousins and other extended family in front of an apartment complex on Roscoe Boulevard in Panorama City in 1989. (Courtesy of Allan Aquino.)

Over the decades, school dances have become sites and rituals for youth expression. Seen here is a group of friends prior to attending St. Genevieve's homecoming dance in 1989. (Courtesy of Aileen Domingo Paras.)

Aileen Domingo Paras gets ready for a party by using hairspray to hold her hair up, as was the style for Filipino American youths during the late 1980s. Aqua Net hairspray became a symbol of 1980s fashion as pomade did generations earlier. (Courtesy of Aileen Domingo Paras.)

Southern California is the birthplace of skate culture, and the San Fernando Valley was one of the many hotbeds of the local scene. Some young Filipino kids began immersing themselves in skateboarding beginning in the 1980s. Butch Velez, who grew up in different places in the Valley, including Arleta, Canoga Park, and Northridge, is pictured here at Hansen Dam Skate Park in Lake View Terrace. (Courtesy of Butch Velez.)

These friends made up the group Bahay Tribe. The dance crew performed at many Filipino parties and events throughout Southern California during the early 1990s. Pictured above are the ladies of Bahay Tribe in Reseda; from left to right are Emilie Padua-Douglas, Therese Quiambao Annes, Liza Makabenta Sacilioc, Anne Jureidini, and Maite Zabala-Alday, with Roland Ramos kneeling in front. Below are the male members of the group at a Northridge home; pictured from left to right are Pierre DeCastro, Audwin Joya, Mark Factora, Jonathan Zabala, Nick Del Rosario, Lawrence Molina, and Roland Ramos. (Both, courtesy of Liza Makabenta Sacilioc.)

Many young Filipino Americans immersed themselves in a car subculture developed in Southern California where enthusiasts modified Japanese cars as an Asian American answer to lowrider and muscle car traditions. As a controversial space to assert Asian male masculinity, the import car scene became incredibly popular, spawning films such as the Fast and the Furious franchise. The Valley was a hotbed of this scene, with drivers racing them legally and illegally while others simply enjoyed their aesthetic style. Many times, car owners all over the Valley and beyond would gather in Sun Valley (at the intersection of Roscoe Boulevard and Coldwater Canyon Avenue), then find wide-open streets to drag race. Here are a couple of these cars in a Valley industrial parking lot, and below is Brian Tiongson-Reyes in his Honda Civic in the mid-1990s. (Both, courtesy of Max Reyes.)

Loitering on the street next to their vehicles was a common sight among young teens in the residential neighborhoods of the San Fernando Valley during the 1990s. Here, young teen Audwin Joya stands in front of an Acura Integra in Canoga Park during an evening. (Courtesy of Liza Makabenta Sacilioc.)

Roland Ramos sits in his car in Reseda with a *yosi*, or cigarette in Tagalog slang. He and his friends were getting ready for a fun day at Disneyland in 1992. (Courtesy of Liza Makabenta Sacilioc.)

Formals and school dances have evolved over the centuries from aristocratic balls during Enlightenment-era Europe to the iconic rite of passage for teenagers at American high schools. These rituals are highly anticipated and exciting social events. In Filipino tradition, a "debut," or debutante ball, is a celebration of a woman's 18th birthday dating back to the Spanish colonial period, when elite Philippine families "presented" their daughters to the community. Modern debuts include a choreographed cotillion dance and a presentation of 18 roses from close friends. Ballrooms and community halls throughout the Valley have served as venues for these celebrations. Seen here is the debut of Melissa Ochoa at the Castaway in Burbank in 1994. Below, young gentlemen pose for photographs in Panorama City before a school dance during the mid-1990s. (Above, courtesy of the Ochoa family; below, courtesy of Mara Shinn Smith.)

The San Fernando Valley and mall culture were synonymous in popular culture as Hollywood writers observed local teenagers. At the height of American mall culture during the 1980s and 1990s, many young Filipino Americans in the Valley flocked to local shopping malls as a place to see and be seen. Here are Christine Gonzales (left) and Rachel Ner trying on shoes at the Northridge Mall in 1996. (Courtesy of Rachel DeGuzman.)

Edward Santos (left) and Danny Cometa are seen in a candid shot during the mid-1990s. Their appearance reflects young teen fashion among many Filipino Americans during the time. (Courtesy of Rachel DeGuzman.)

As hip-hop became more popular during the 1980s, many Filipino Americans up and down the West Coast embodied the art form and participated in the culture. Filipinos found a particular niche as DJs and turntablists, forming DJ crews and performing in mainstream hip-hop venues with legendary artists. Here is Edward Santos practicing in a backyard in Winnetka during the mid-1990s. (Courtesy of Rachel DeGuzman.)

During the 1990s and 2000s, many youths of color in California frequented photography studios at local malls. Studios like Glamour Shots and Photo Makers were popular with teenagers as they offered photography sessions for a relatively affordable fee. The photographs often featured a hazy glow and backgrounds, resulting in a stylized blurry tone. This is a group shot of Filipino American couples taken at a studio. (Courtesy of Rachel DeGuzman.)

Among many youths who grew up with large extended families, cousins are people's "first friends." Above are the Ochoa cousins and friends gathering on the porch of their house in North Hollywood for Christmas in 2002. Below are the Viray and De Mira cousins gathering at a residence in Pacoima in 2019. (Above, courtesy of the Ochoa family; below, courtesy of Carl Angelo Viray.)

Colleges and universities, especially on the West Coast, experienced increased enrollment of Filipino students as many children of immigrants came of age beginning in the 1980s. In 1981, students at California State University, Northridge, organized the Filipino American Student Association, which provides a social and cultural outlet for students looking for camaraderie and belonging. Pictured is a FASA gathering at Northridge Park in 1994. (Courtesy of Aileen Domingo Paras.)

Sportsfest is an annual sports event hosted by California State Polytechnic University–Pomona's Filipino student club, Barkada, where Filipino college organizations throughout California gather to compete in basketball, softball, tennis, and other sports tournaments. Here are members of FASA's softball team posing on Cal Poly Pomona's playing fields in 1995. (Courtesy of Aileen Domingo Paras.)

Filipino American college students are gathered on the campus of California State University, Northridge, in 1988 during the halftime performances of the annual Northridge Invitational Tournament (NIT), organized by FASA. The sports event began in 1986 to bring together local Filipino American college organizations through sports competitions. Below are members of FASA posing in front of their winning trophy in 1996. (Above, courtesy of Nenette Tenza-Umali; below, courtesy of Moonie Lantion.)

Joe Casuga of the Filipino American Student Association throws a softball at Cal State Northridge's Matador Field during practice for the annual Sportsfest. Sports competitions between different Filipino college clubs were an opportune time to meet other Filipino American youths across California. (Courtesy of Moonie Lantion.)

During the 1980s, Los Angeles Pierce College in Woodland Hills, like other schools, experienced an influx of Filipino community college students. In 1990, a group of Filipinos established the Kabataang Filipino Club. Pierce College also had a couple of Filipino American college presidents lead the school in its history: E. Bing Inocencio and Alexis Montevirgen. Pictured here is a gathering of club members in 1991. (Courtesy of Janel Santos Kalaw.)

Students attend a club general meeting at Pierce College in 1992. Organizing student activities was more difficult in community colleges than in traditional university settings. Nonetheless, Filipinos were successful at making the Kabataang Filipino Club thrive during the 1990s. (Courtesy of Janel Santos Kalaw.)

Members of Pierce College's Kabataang Filipino Club threw many parties, which attracted many young Filipinos from all over the Valley and beyond. Here, young Filipino college students enjoy a slow dance at a Valentine's Day party called "A Night to Remember," held at the Best Western in Canoga Park in 1991. (Courtesy of Janel Santos Kalaw.)

During the early 1990s, the growing Filipino student population at Los Angeles Valley College (LAVC) organized the Pilipino United Student Organization (PUSO). Here is a photograph of student leader John Mina waiting to speak at a Filipino cultural event at the LAVC campus. Below is a group picture of the student organization. (Both, courtesy of John Mina.)

A growing movement of Filipino Americans learning about their ethnic identity emerged during the 1990s, largely due to increased numbers of second-generation Filipino Americans entering college and taking ethnic studies courses. Here are, from left to right, Lance Dougherty, Moonie Lantion, Jojo Abuan, and Allan Aquino after facilitating a workshop on Filipino history and identity at CSUN in October 1996. The workshop was part of the first Students for Pilipino American History Month (SPAHM), an annual series of events at CSUN. (Courtesy of Allan Aquino.)

Jocelyn Enriquez, a popular Filipina American R&B/freestyle artist, performed her hit song "A Little Bit of Ecstasy" at the CSUN University Student Union during FASA's inaugural SPAHM Noontime Concert in 1997. The event attracted hundreds of CSUN students and other youths in the community. (Courtesy of Allan Aquino.)

Pilipino Cultural Night (PCN) is a staple institution among Filipino American college organizations throughout the nation. Since the early 1970s, when they were first conceptualized, PCNs evolved into stage productions that feature Philippine cultural dances, hip-hop performances, and dramatic plays that convey life for Filipino American youth. CSUN staged its first PCN in 1986. Preparation for the event begins months prior. Here are FASA students practicing for their dance performances on top of a parking structure, which was eventually demolished by the 1994 Northridge Earthquake. (Both, courtesy of Moonie Lantion.)

Pilipino Cultural Night continues to be a college tradition among Filipino Americans in the United States. Here is a picture of CSUN students performing the staged play portion of the production in 2019, and below is a photograph taken during the cast curtain call. (Both, courtesy of Filipino American Student Association, California State University, Northridge.)

Pilipino Graduation, or "P-Grad," is a special ceremony held on many campuses throughout the United States honoring Filipino American graduates. The ceremony usually includes graduates wearing a Philippine flag-inspired stole and giving personal speeches thanking their family and friends. The first P-Grad was celebrated at California State University, Northridge, in 1998. Seen here is CSUN's Filipino graduating class of 2019. (Courtesy of Filipino American Student Association, California State University, Northridge.)

Four

Making Space and Place in the Valley

Many urban planners today shun the sprawled suburban development of the Valley as an archaic relic of the past that should never be replicated. Suburban sprawl has certainly caused considerable environmental damage and nightmarish traffic. Even more pervasive, perceptions of the lack of communal "third spaces" and of monotony and conformity have overshadowed suburbia's cultural impact. As these characterizations of the San Fernando Valley and other suburban spaces gain momentum in national discourse, they suspiciously coincide with its increasing diversification. Suburbia has changed considerably since the mid-20th century. Current suburban experiences, as many scholars argue, have complicated such harsh cultural critiques, and yet the prevailing popular tenet concerning suburbia is that it perpetuates spatial homogeneity.

After decades of integration, Filipinos and other communities of color have remade suburban spaces to fit their own needs. In many ways, they implicitly challenged the heteronormative, nuclear family ethos that suburban architecture tries to discipline. With larger, multi-generational families living in the home, extensions and additional units had to be strategically created in the single-family home. Many Filipinos converted their backyards to full-scale gardens to grow native Philippine fruits and vegetables. Youths converted car garages into dance floors for large parties. Living rooms became performance stages for karaoke sessions. Outside of the home, Filipinos created quasi-public institutions across the Valley. Strip malls became sites where Filipino businesses could thrive, and patrons gathered. Many Catholic and Protestant churches that once had predominantly white congregations quickly became majority Filipino, changing the rituals of communal worship. These are but a few examples of how Filipino Americans made a place in the San Fernando Valley.

The challenge, of course, is where to find these subtle examples of Filipino placemaking. There's still a real perception that Filipinos are invisible in the region. Where can one find Filipinos in such sprawl and conformity? The Philippines' colonial legacy created an English-speaking Filipino American population where the community could blend into the American suburban landscape because of geographic dispersion, institutional integration, and aesthetic assimilation. Like the San Fernando Valley itself, a symbol of anonymity where Hollywood could make the region seem everywhere and nowhere at the same time, Filipinos blend in seamlessly. Yet Filipinos could be seen. One just needed to know where to look. By uncovering these places and shedding light on specific hidden spaces in the Valley, this chapter hopes to convey how Filipino Americans made space everywhere out of nowhere.

Without a notable landmark, the San Fernando Valley Boosters had difficulty in marketing the Valley as a destination. In this postcard from the 1950s, the Valley is depicted in its seemingly endless sprawl and car-centric Ventura Boulevard. Yet, in the vastness of this perceived culturally barren landscape, Filipinos' presence can certainly be found. (Courtesy of San Fernando Valley Digital History Library/Special Collections and Archives, University Library, California State University, Northridge.)

As post-1965 Filipino Americans began moving to suburban homes in the Valley during the 1970s, individual homes began reflecting and demonstrating a unique Filipino American aesthetic. This is the kitchen of Antonio and Virgie Cruz in Canoga Park, where the image of Jesus's Last Supper, a quintessential Filipino Catholic adornment, hovers above while a Mickey Mouse clock conveys Filipinos' long history with American popular culture. (Courtesy of the Cruz family.)

As Filipinos migrated to the Valley in large numbers, they brought a particular Filipino aesthetic to the Valley's mid-century homes. Here is an example of a house decorated with Tinikling dancers adorned on the wall at the Layba family home in Winnetka. Pictured from left to right are Gudelia Malicdem, Illuminada Layba, Sulo Lolita Layba, Godfrey Malicdem, and Miel Layba. (Courtesy of Mina Layba.)

Dancing is a significant part of Filipino life. Throughout the history of Americanization, Filipinos have been particularly keen on performing the latest dances that emerge in popular culture. Here is the Leviste living room converted to an impromptu dance floor during a party in the 1970s. (Courtesy of the Leviste family.)

The living room of Tagumpay de Leon's home in Burbank is the site of this 1986 mini-concert of the FilAm Family Cultural Group, a cultural arts organization founded by Betty Friese that promoted Philippine dance and music and whose members hailed from different parts of Southern California. Pictured from left to right are Nitoy Gonzales, Tagumpay de Leon, Jovita Sison-Friese, Grace Kucera, and Elvie Au (singer). (Courtesy of Lakandiwa de Leon.)

In newly acquired homes, Filipino Americans across the suburban San Fernando Valley used patios as communal spaces for gatherings. In many instances, Filipinos would enclose the patio and convert it into an additional indoor room in their house to accommodate their expanding families. The Vela family hosts friends and relatives on the outdoor patio of their Reseda home around the late 1980s. (Courtesy of Vanessa Vela-Lovelace.)

In Filipino Catholic tradition, families call upon a priest to bless a new home for good fortune and prosperity. These ceremonies entail going from room to room to sprinkle holy water and reciting prayers. They exemplify the mixture of Catholicism and indigenous Philippine spiritual practices that have amalgamated throughout centuries of colonial rule. The tradition lives on among many Filipinos throughout the global diaspora. This image was captured during a house blessing at the Dolalas home in North Hills during the early 1980s. Below, Calixtus Dolalas throws coins up into the air for abundance, with his nieces and nephews eagerly awaiting his gesture of generosity. (Both, courtesy of Elaine Dolalas.)

Among many Filipinos, the home is as much of a spiritual place as the church. Sections of the house are transformed into altars or spiritual areas. Various statues of Mary, Jesus, or patron saints adorn these spaces. Pictured are Joey and Cely Salanga standing with Norma Mina in front of a grotto with the Virgin Mary statue in the backyard of the Minas' Burbank home. (Courtesy of Nathaniel V. Mina.)

Block rosary is a Filipino tradition where communities gather to pray the rosary. The ritual involves passing a Virgin Mary statue to different households for daily prayer. Matriarchs of the host families usually lead the rosary, reminiscent of precolonial culture when women served as spiritual leaders. Many Filipinos at American Catholic churches organize block rosary groups, including this group at the Dolalas household in North Hills. (Courtesy of Elaine Dolalas.)

With large extended families, many Filipinos opt to use their home garages as another gathering space during parties. Pictured here is the Shinn family socializing in their garage in the early 1990s. (Courtesy of Mara Shinn Smith.)

In a privatized suburban landscape, many youths were creative in reusing backyards and garages as dance floors. This is a garage party at the Domingo house in Northridge in 1990. (Courtesy of Aileen Domingo Paras.)

Where yards had once been utilitarian spaces, with kitchen gardens and sometimes farm animals, the suburban yard differed and became a status symbol of American life. Manicured lawns and decorative gardens in the yard aimed to convey middle-class tranquility. Many Filipinos practiced such principles upon their arrival to suburbia. In this image, Teresita Veluz tends to her roses at her Van Nuys home in 1984. (Courtesy of Melissa Veluz.)

With ample backyard space, many Filipinos in the San Fernando Valley who had experience growing their own food in the Philippines took the opportunity to create gardens to grow Filipino vegetables in their home. Seen here are Carlos Veluz and Carlos Jr. tending their vegetable garden in the backyard of their newly purchased Van Nuys home in 1982. (Courtesy of Melissa Veluz.)

As former agricultural land, many homes in the Valley came with fruit trees and had fertile soil for new vegetation to grow and thrive. Teresita Veluz enjoys the fruits of their backyard plum tree, while from left to right, her children Melissa, Carlos Jr., also known as "Charlie," and Rhoda enjoy climbing the natural jungle gym in 1982. (Courtesy of Melissa Veluz.)

Many Filipinos were able to plant and grow tropical fruit trees in their new Valley backyards. Celia de la Cruz and her daughter Annabelle pose behind the new guava tree they planted in their backyard in Panorama City. (Courtesy of the de la Cruz family.)

Swimming pools in the backyard, a real estate selling point that marked privatized suburban living, became synonymous with housing in the San Fernando Valley. To provide some relief from extremely hot days in the San Fernando Valley, residents kept cool and enjoyed recreational activities in pools that dotted the Valley's landscape. The Vela family enjoys playing in the pool of their Reseda home in the late 1980s. (Courtesy of Vanessa Vela-Lovelace.)

Backyard parties are a staple in the suburban landscape. Many youths use the space to throw parties with a DJ at the helm. Seen here are a few partygoers attending a Northridge backyard birthday party in 1990. (Courtesy of Aileen Domingo Paras.)

With a huge population boom in Panorama City after World War II, the Los Angeles Archdiocese established St. Genevieve's Parish on Roscoe Boulevard in 1950. By the 1980s, the demographic makeup of the parish changed dramatically as Filipinos and Latinos moved into the area. St. Genevieve's has the highest concentration of Filipino parishioners in the Valley, making the parish the epicenter of Filipino Catholic and social life in the region. (Author's collection.)

Our Lady of the Valley Church is among the oldest churches in the San Fernando Valley. Built in 1921, the church served as the lone Catholic church for the sparsely populated western part of the Valley. Like all of the Valley, the church grew after post–World War II suburban housing was built. By the 1980s and 1990s, Filipino Americans flocked to the parish as more settled in Canoga Park and surrounding neighborhoods. (Author's collection.)

Iglesia Ni Cristo, which translates to Church of Christ, is the largest Protestant church in the Philippines and was founded by Felix Manalo in 1914. In 1986, local Valley members of the church began to organize a congregation. In 1992, this Gothic-style church on Nordhoff Street in Panorama City opened its doors to the community. The church has since grown to several hundred members with two congregations in the Valley. (Author's collection.)

The Filipino International Fellowship Church, another Protestant congregation catering to Filipino Americans in the San Fernando Valley, was founded in Van Nuys in 1989 by Pastor Edgar Florendo. It has since moved to share space with the Northridge Christian Church in Northridge. (Author's collection.)

Our Lady of Lourdes Catholic Church was established in 1958, when Northridge was predominantly white. As the parish grew and diversified, it erected a welcoming sign to the diverse communities of Northridge. (Author's collection.)

Church festivals are regular occurrences across the Valley that galvanize parishioners in supporting the local churches. The annual St. Genevieve Fiesta brings together the parish community and neighbors throughout Panorama City. In this image, Elvessa Dolalas and young Elaine are at the fiesta in 1985. (Courtesy of Elaine Dolalas.)

Panorama Recreation Center was part of the originally planned community of Panorama City when it was developed in the late 1940s. Adjacent to Chase Elementary School, the park is called "Chase Park" among locals. On most days, the park's basketball court is filled with hoopers of all ages playing the Philippines' most popular sport. The tennis courts, on the other side of the park, also serve as a social and recreation site for mostly middle-aged and senior Filipinos, particularly during the morning hours. (Both, author's collection.)

John Quimby Park in Canoga Park is another recreation space for the growing Filipino American community in the west San Fernando Valley to play pick-up basketball. Weekend mornings are especially popular among Pinoys who are just getting off of their night shifts. (Author's collection.)

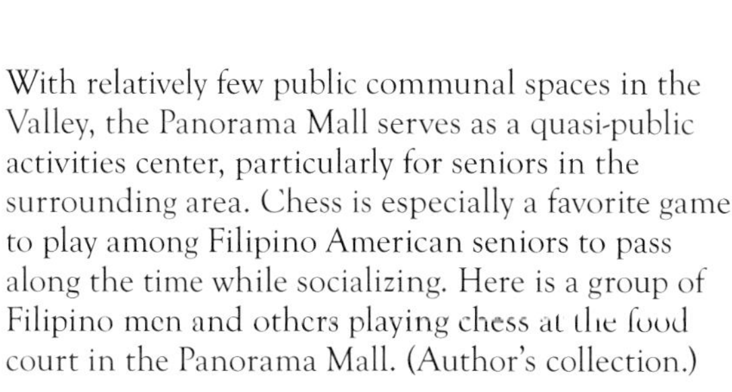

With relatively few public communal spaces in the Valley, the Panorama Mall serves as a quasi-public activities center, particularly for seniors in the surrounding area. Chess is especially a favorite game to play among Filipino American seniors to pass along the time while socializing. Here is a group of Filipino men and others playing chess at the food court in the Panorama Mall. (Author's collection.)

As perhaps the only global entertainment destination in the region, Universal Studios attracts people from all over the world to the San Fernando Valley. Tourists and local residents alike enjoy visiting the park to take a peek at "movie magic." Adoracion Corpus Barretto (left), Leni Barretto Shinn, and baby Mara Shinn Smith are pictured at Universal Studios in 1974. (Courtesy of Mara Shinn Smith.)

From left to right, Sonia Sawit, Rayson Esquejo, Sheryl Beran, and Neny Sawit ride the famous Universal Studios Tram Tour. The tour is one of the few places where the general public can visit current and historical film sets and learn how some of their favorite movies are made. (Courtesy of Rayson Esquejo.)

Teresita Veluz and her children, from left to right, Rhoda, Carlos "Charlie" Jr., and Melissa pose in front of the famous giant telephone at the former Prop Plaza at Universal Studios during the 1980s. The phone was used in the movies *The Incredible Shrinking Man* and *Land of the Giants*. (Courtesy of Melissa Veluz.)

Opened in 1993, Universal CityWalk is an urban entertainment complex built on a hilltop adjacent to Universal Studios. The privatized outdoor mall became an entertainment hub for many Valley residents, particularly among youths and families, becoming a prototype for many outdoor entertainment centers. Among Filipino Americans, CityWalk was a place to bring visiting relatives or a destination for young teenagers looking for fun. (Courtesy of the Ochoa family.)

Since the early 20th century, Southern California has been the aviation and aerospace hub of the United States. The industry was a vital economic engine for the entire region, including the San Fernando Valley, spawning a particular aviation culture, including air shows. Jessica Leviste sits on the airfield at Burbank Airport to watch an air show during the 1970s. (Courtesy of the Leviste family.)

The Van Nuys Air National Guard Base was a former military base located at Van Nuys Airport. Built during World War II, the base closed after the federal government cut defense spending following the end of the Cold War. Jomari Arciaga is pictured with his daughter Selyna, his friend Ramon Naval, and Ramon's son Ian in front of an F-15 Eagle shortly after the base closure. (Courtesy of Jomari Arciaga.)

With a relative lack of public space in the San Fernando Valley, playgrounds at McDonald's restaurants are a ubiquitous sight across the Valley. These private playgrounds served, and continue to serve, as spaces of recreation for young children. Seen here is young Mara Shinn Smith on the slide at the McDonald's location on Woodman Avenue and Osborne Street during the late 1970s. (Courtesy of Mara Shinn Smith.)

From left to right, young cousins Michelle Ochoa-Veluz McGrudder, Joe Ochoa, and Mike Ochoa-Veluz enjoy a fun day at Castle Park in Sherman Oaks in 1986. Castle Park originally opened in 1976 as a miniature golf course. Its owners converted it into a full family amusement center during the 1980s. Castle Park continues to operate today, attracting families all over the San Fernando Valley. (Courtesy of the Ochoa family.)

Established in 1970, the Odyssey Restaurant on top of Odyssey Hill in Granada Hills has served as an important event space for many people in the Valley. Countless Filipino Americans have celebrated birthday parties, weddings, debuts (debutante balls), association installation dinners, and other gatherings at the Odyssey. A group of friends celebrates the wedding of Ging and Carol Altamira in June 1981. (Courtesy of Erwin Altamira.)

From left to right, Melanie Esteban Black, Michele Esteban Mendoza, and Jessica Leviste are pictured in front of the Broadway department store at the Topanga Plaza Mall during the mid-1980s. Topanga Plaza opened in 1964 and has been a shopping destination for many Valley residents for decades. Topanga Plaza's food hall, which opened in 2023, features a couple of Filipino-owned shops, including Wanderlust Creamery. (Courtesy of the Leviste family.)

Members of CSUN FASA enjoy a night out at the Iceoplex during the mid-1990s. The North Hills ice skating facility opened in 1992 amidst the surge in popularity of hockey in Southern California after Wayne Gretzky joined the Los Angeles Kings NHL hockey team in 1988. The Iceoplex closed in 2001 and relocated to nearby Simi Valley. (Courtesy of Aileen Domingo Paras.)

Many Filipino students at Pierce College used to loiter between classes around an area under what they called the "Manila Tree," or just "the Tree." According to oral histories, this practice of *tambay*, or loitering at this location, began in the early 1980s and continued for decades. Here are some Filipino students at the tree in 1991. (Courtesy of Janel Santos Kalaw.)

The Glenn Omatsu House, formerly known as the Asian House when it opened in 1992, serves as a meeting and gathering place for Asian American student organizations at California State University, Northridge, including the Filipino American Student Association. The house is just north of the CSUN campus at 18356 Halsted Street. Below is a group of Filipino organizers at the Asian House in 1997. (Above, author's collection; below, courtesy of Moonie Lantion.)

Established in 1797, the San Fernando Rey de España Mission marks Spain's first colonial venture in the area and gave the San Fernando Valley its name. As a functioning church, the San Fernando Mission has also hosted countless weddings of Filipino Americans. This is a picture of a wedding party as they line up just outside of the church during the late 1990s. (Courtesy of the Cruz family.)

Thousands of Filipino Americans have their final resting place in Mission Hills at the San Fernando Mission Cemetery, the only Catholic cemetery in the Valley. Pictured is the burial ceremony of Reynaldo Banzali Estrada in 1983. (Courtesy of Marie and Reanne Estrada.)

Lady Munchies opened as one of the first Filipino karaoke restaurants in the Valley in the mid-1980s. Celita de Castro owned the popular late-night spot in a Sun Valley strip mall at the intersection of Roscoe and Laurel Canyon Boulevards. Many talented singers came to Lady Munchies to sing, eventually sparking the idea of creating a boy band in the 1980s. De Castro brought together singers who frequented the restaurant and created A.D.O.B.O. (A Dose of Brown Origin), and later a female counterpart, SSSHe (Sexy, Sensual, Seductive, Hyper). Both bands toured around Southern California and beyond. Lady Munchies closed its doors a few years later. This is the interior of the restaurant with Alma Albancio (left) and Ninette Tenza-Umali on the karaoke stage, and below are friends gathered in the parking lot in front of the restaurant. (Both, courtesy of Ninette Tenza-Umali.)

Ultimate was a DJ crew started by Arian Leviste, Jerome Lorenzo, and Jeffrey Monasterial during the mid-1980s. In 1990, they opened a storefront in Reseda where they would rent out sound and lighting equipment in addition to their regular DJ gigs. Pictured here is a group of friends with the Ultimate Crew in 1990, and below is the storefront in 2024. (Above, courtesy of Aileen Domingo Paras; below, author's collection.)

Among the largest Filipino supermarket chains in the United States, Island Pacific Supermarket began in the San Fernando Valley with its first store in Panorama City in March 2000. Founded by CEO Nino Jefferson Lim, the Panorama City location on Roscoe Boulevard and Van Nuys Boulevard promoted Filipino cuisine and products to the communities of the San Fernando Valley. Within the store was the Kababayan Center, a mini-mall that housed several Filipino-owned businesses and restaurants, including a community center. The supermarket also hosted many community events and Filipino star appearances throughout the years. Unfortunately, Island Pacific closed the Panorama City store in 2018, but it continues to serve the Filipino community with dozens of locations throughout California and Nevada, including its other San Fernando Valley stores in Canoga Park and Granada Hills (exterior and interior pictured). (Both, author's collection.)

D.J. Bibingkahan is a popular *turo-turo* restaurant where Filipino dishes are served cafeteria style, a model ubiquitous to most Filipino restaurants in the United States. The Feliciano family opened its original location in Panorama City across the street from Kaiser Permanente Hospital. The restaurant expanded to several locations throughout Southern California, including Carson, Artesia, West Covina, central Los Angeles, and Vallejo in Northern California and Las Vegas. (Author's collection.)

Oi Asian Fusion, a popular rice bowl restaurant, first opened in a small eight-seater storefront in Reseda in 2013. After quickly outgrowing its first location, owner and chef Eric De La Cruz moved the restaurant to a location in Canoga Park. Oi Asian Fusion now has multiple locations across Southern California. (Author's collection.)

Collective Lifestyle, a streetwear fashion store, opened its store on Reseda Boulevard in 2015. C.J. Berina, a native of the San Fernando Valley and graduate of CSUN, launched the space, bringing fashion, music, art, and live events like open mic nights and weekend festivals to the heart of Northridge, helping to redefine the Valley from a bedroom community to an artistic hub through creativity and placemaking. (Courtesy of C.J. Berina.)

Café Aficionado is a family-owned coffee shop in Northridge. Owned by Reggie and Abigail Cua, the shop also serves as a gathering spot and hosts many collaborative pop-up markets, including a Filipino American History Month community event in October. (Author's collection.)

Boba tea is a tea-based drink that originated in Taiwan in the early 1980s. Boba shops became popular among Asian American teenagers in the 1990s and 2000s as a place to socialize. Filipino entrepreneurs began opening up shops that sold the drink but also offered traditional Filipino dessert drinks like *halo halo* and *taho*. Here are some of the owners of Craft Tea House, a popular shop in Panorama City. (Author's collection.)

Kristine de la Cruz opened Créme Caramel in Sherman Oaks after selling her version of leche flan and other Filipino desserts at farmer's markets throughout Southern California, which quickly became popular. This is the bakery on Kester Avenue. (Courtesy of Kristine de la Cruz.)

The Filipino collection at the Panorama City branch of the Los Angeles Public Library is one of a few such highlighted ethnic literature collections in the local library system. Located in the same plaza as many other Filipino establishments on Roscoe and Van Nuys Boulevards, the library branch attracts many Filipino youth and seniors looking for literary resources. (Author's collection.)

The intersection of Roscoe Boulevard and Woodman Avenue has served as the historic heart of the Filipino American community in Panorama City for decades. With the Kaiser Hospital across the street, many Filipino establishments have taken advantage of the numerous Filipino consumers who work as medical staff. Though some have come and gone, many businesses continue to vie for space in the handful of commercial strip malls within the vicinity. (Author's collection.)

Five

Faces and Stories from Filipino American Suburbia

Cultural critics say nothing happens in suburbia. In addition to its physical and architectural appearance, culture in suburban areas is usually met with condescension. Conformity, monotony, and predictability are the usual adjectives that describe the suburbs, and the San Fernando Valley continues to bear the brunt of this disparagement (that, and being too damn hot during the summer). Yet, over the last 50 years, the Valley, and American suburbia in general, has changed dramatically. Integration, immigration, and housing unaffordability have created a more racially and economically diverse suburban landscape, mirroring the urban cities. The Valley does not possess the attractive beaches of the Westside nor the sense of the history of downtown Los Angeles, but it does have its own unique culture, history, and cadre of changemakers. Events have occurred in the Valley that have shaped the greater region despite the absence of media attention and the relative anonymity of life in the suburbs.

For Filipino Americans, 78,477 call the San Fernando Valley home in 2020, and many more have passed through during their lifetimes. Each one of them has their own stories shaped in this unique environment. There are communities bound together through pain and love and moments that may or may not have been captured by a camera. Many Filipinos have emerged to become changemakers in their respective fields, forging new paths for others. It was not an easy path to be sure. Political and media representation continue to remain elusive for Filipino Americans, making the stories of Filipinos in the San Fernando Valley largely obscured and suppressed. There are many historical and global reasons for this omission. Yet the stories exist, and it is imperative to collect, document, and retell them over and over.

It is impossible to document every life and story of the close to 80,000 Filipino Americans (and more) in the San Fernando Valley. Nevertheless, this final chapter of the book is an attempt to highlight just a few of those stories that have emerged in the community and some of the inspirational and creative people who have ignited a brighter world. Many photographs in this chapter are linked in some form to larger histories and cultures, and collectively, they represent the vibrancy and hope in the so-called boring and desolate suburbs. Although these photographs only provide a small glimpse of the stories and people of the Valley, there is much more that lies beyond the frame.

Tagumpay de Leon is a world-renowned musician and performer of *rondalla*, a Philippine music form with Spanish influences comprised of stringed instruments. De Leon migrated to America in 1971 and eventually settled in Burbank. In 2021, he was named a National Heritage Fellow by the National Endowment for the Arts (NEA). Here is de Leon (left) playing with Philippine music legend Nitoy Gonzales in 1986. (Courtesy of Lakandiwa de Leon.)

Malaya Filipino American Dance Arts is an ensemble of performing artists, dancers, and musicians based in Los Angeles's San Fernando Valley. It was founded in 2012 by executive director Anna Lisa Gutierrez De Guzman and artistic director Peter De Guzman (pictured here). Since its founding, it has become one of the premier Philippine dance arts companies in Southern California, helping to redefine Philippine dance for future generations of Filipino Americans. (Courtesy of Malaya Filipino American Dance Arts.)

Filipino Martial Arts practitioner Guro Michael Makabenta trained and taught at the Magda Institute in Reseda for many years before forming his own school in Granada Hills with the blessing and guidance of Pamana Kali founder Guro Alvin Catacutan. Valley native Makabenta has taught countless people Philippine heritage and culture through Filipino Martial Arts as well as other Asian martial arts styles. Pamana Kali–San Fernando Valley, which trains at a Filipino-owned Pilates studio on Chatsworth Street, continues to grow and thrive. Above, Makabenta teaches a young student the practice of striking and defending with a long blade. Below, students participate in sparring with practice sticks. (Both, courtesy of Pamana Kali–San Fernando Valley.)

Guro Janel Barlongo is a Filipino Martial Arts (FMA) instructor based in the San Fernando Valley. As a college student at CSUN, she was exposed to the martial art by Guro Dan Inosanto, a pioneer of FMA in the United States, who gave a workshop on campus. After training under various teachers, she eventually began teaching on her own at Evolution Martial Arts in Chatsworth. (Courtesy of Janel Barlongo.)

Adrienne Borlongan and J.P. Lopez grew up in the Valley and attended CSUN. In 2015, they opened Wanderlust Creamery, an artisanal ice cream shop specializing in flavors inspired by world travel, in Tarzana. They have since opened numerous locations throughout Southern California, becoming one of the most popular independent ice cream shops in the nation. Honoring their heritage, they consistently offer an array of Filipino flavors. (Courtesy of Adrienne Borlongan.)

Gina Lopez Alexander is a designer who created a line of handbags and other kinds of accessories. She began her business in 1999 in her Burbank home to fund her daughter's adoption, and it soon blossomed into a multimillion-dollar enterprise. The late Los Angeles Lakers star Kobe Bryant became one of her star clients, purchasing her handbags for his wife and daughters. (Courtesy of Gina Lopez Alexander.)

Cecile and Dante Ochoa are veteran journalists who have worked in the Philippines and in the United States. They immigrated during the 1970s and settled in North Hollywood. Disillusioned by the lack of quality journalism to service the community, the Ochoas launched several publications from their home to capture the stories of Filipino Americans locally and nationally. They have also authored numerous books and countless articles. (Courtesy of Cecile Ochoa.)

Alisa Damaso is a Pinay graphic designer, illustrator, letterer, writer, and founder of VLY GRL. With the pervasive "Valley Girl" stereotype dominating the public imagination, Damaso created the line of fun accessories and apparel with a mission to smash the narrative of the bimbo Valley Girl. Here is Damaso promoting and selling her products during a community arts event at Reseda Park. (Courtesy of Alisa Damaso.)

Tattooing has a long history in the Philippines, dating back centuries before the colonial era. Charlyn Quirino Vega is a tattoo artist and owner of Queens of Needles in Northridge. When she was 14, she moved to the San Fernando Valley, where she first practiced graffiti art and then eventually tattooing. Here is Vega in her studio creating a Dodger tattoo on a client. (Courtesy of Char Vega.)

Butch Velez, also known as "Tracer One," and Johnny Luna, also known as "Type," are Filipinos from the Valley who redefined hip-hop music in the Philippines. In the early 1990s, they moved to the Philippines and created MastaPlann, a hip-hop group with members from Manila and California. They immediately amassed a substantial Philippine and global following. Here, Velez (left) and Luna are overlooking the Valley from Porter Ranch prior to development. (Courtesy of Butch Velez.)

Gaudencio Sillona III, also known as "Jay-R," is a famous singer, songwriter, record producer, and actor in the Philippines. He grew up in Van Nuys and attended St. Genevieve High School in Panorama City. In the early 2000s, he moved to the Philippines and found success in the entertainment industry, becoming the country's "R&B Prince." (Courtesy of Jay-R.)

Addison Magno, also known as "Pare Young," was born in the Philippines and immigrated to the United States in 1999. He lived in different parts of the Valley, including Van Nuys, Panorama City, and North Hills. Magno had a difficult time adjusting to American life and eventually joined the Filipino street gang Jefrox. He was later arrested and incarcerated for 13 years. After his release, he moved back to the Philippines and started a YouTube channel where he documents and complicates the narratives about gang life and criminality among Filipino Americans and other ethnic communities, providing much-needed education for future generations. Another Filipino American who was shaped by the Valley's street environment is hip-hop artist Carl Angelo Viray from North Hills. Here, he is posing in front of his street namesake in Arleta. (Left, courtesy of Addison Magno; below, courtesy of Andrew Celi.)

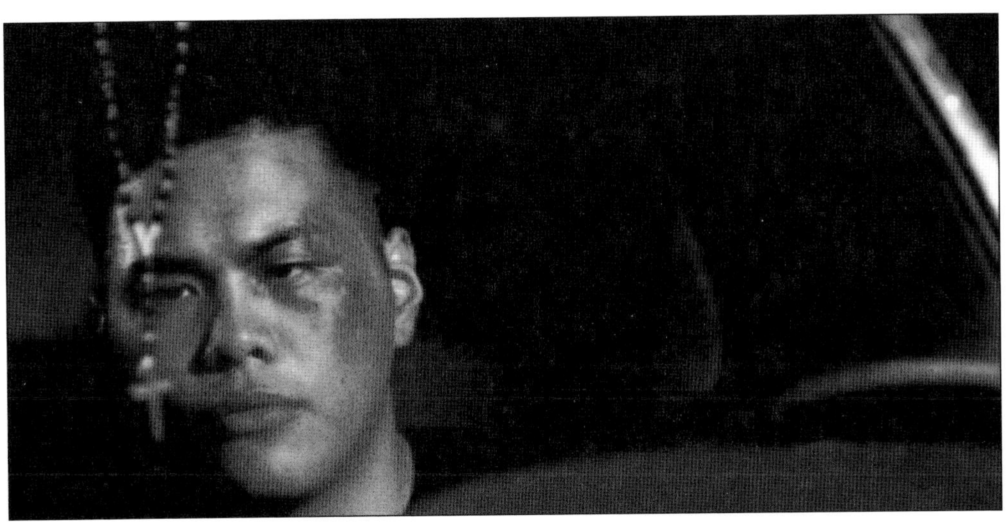

In 2015, Gerardo Maravilla, a Mexican American filmmaker and writer who grew up in the San Fernando Valley, created and produced *CROSS*, a short film about a Filipino American backyard boxer who fights to pay for his mother's medical bills. Inspired by the underground scene of backyard boxing in the Valley and his experience growing up among Mexican Americans and Filipino Americans, Maravilla produces a film that poignantly depicts the real struggles of many communities of color across the working-class neighborhoods of the Valley. Pictured above is the Filipino American lead of the film, Jason Sistona, and below is a still from the movie's big fight scene. (Both, courtesy of Gerardo Maravilla.)

Winfred John Delloro was a national labor leader and community activist, serving as president of the Asian Pacific American Labor Alliance, executive director of the Dolores Huerta Labor Institute, and cofounder of the Pilipino Workers Center. Delloro was born in New Jersey and moved to Northridge at the age of 13. He graduated from Bishop Alemany High School in Mission Hills and attended College of the Canyons and the University of California, Los Angeles, with degrees in psychology and Asian American studies. He dedicated his life to social and economic justice for working people, including helping to organize workers at Northridge Hospital Medical Center and Kaiser Permanente Woodland Hills Medical Center. He sadly passed away in 2010 at the age of 38. At left, Delloro is leading chants at a rally during the early 1990s. Below, he is pictured with his children, Malcolm and Mina. (Both, courtesy of Susan Suh.)

On November 8, 2022, Kenneth Mejia made history as the first Filipino American elected to any office in the City of Los Angeles, as well as the first Asian American elected to any city-wide office when he successfully won his election for city controller. Mejia was born and raised in the San Fernando Valley neighborhood of Sylmar in a single-parent, multi-generational household. He earned his degree in accounting from Woodbury University and received his certified public accountant (CPA) license at the age of 22. After becoming politicized during the 2016 Bernie Sanders presidential campaign, Mejia began organizing working-class communities around tenant rights and ran for several political offices. Mejia, who ran his race for city controller on the platforms of transparency and community accountability, won in a landslide, garnering the most votes in Los Angeles municipal history. (Courtesy of Kenneth Mejia.)

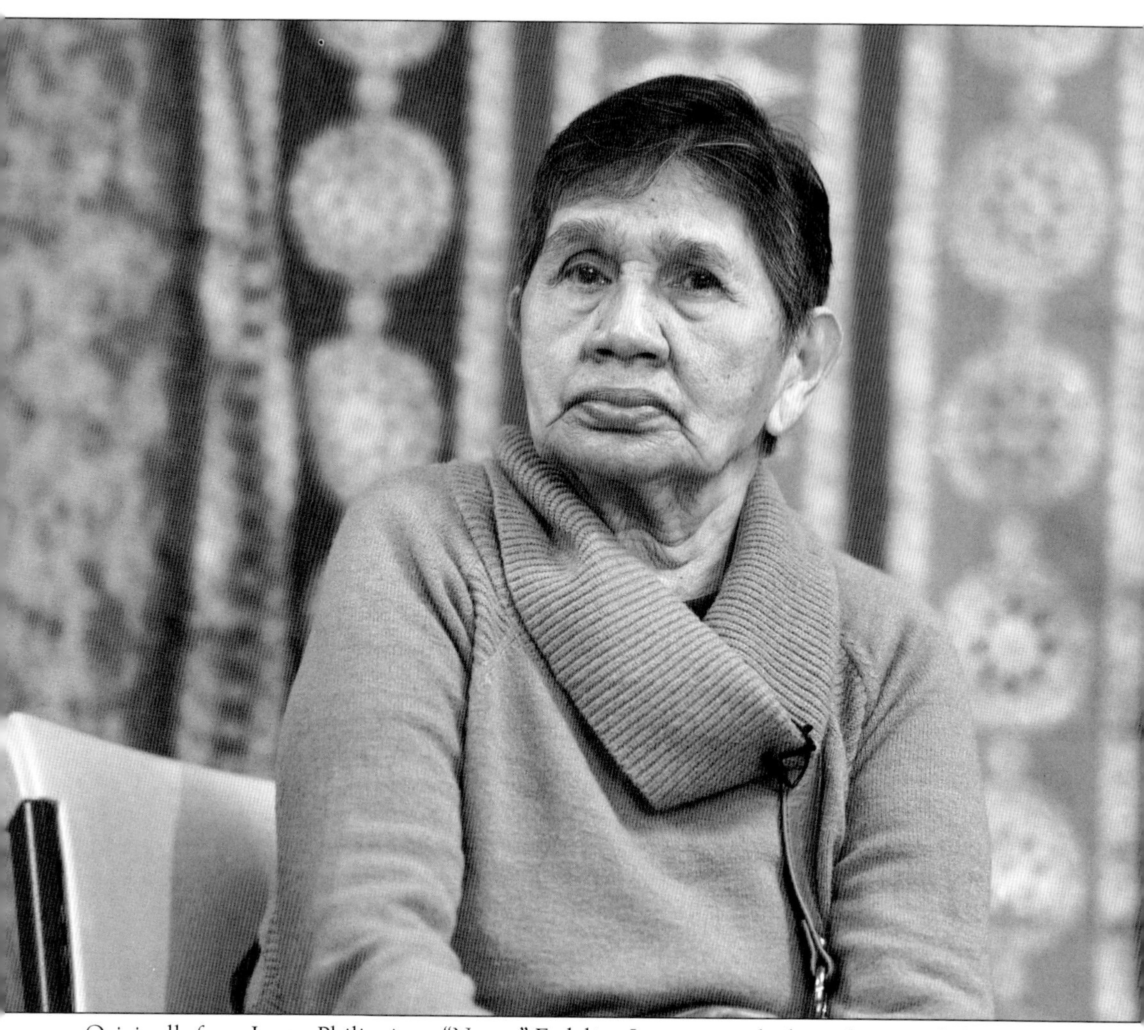

Originally from Leyte, Philippines, "Nanay" Fedelina Lugasan worked as a domestic helper for the family of Benedicta Cox in the Philippines and in Southern California. As a victim of modern-day slavery and human trafficking, Lugasan was not paid for her work cooking, cleaning, and taking care of four generations of Cox's family, nor was she given days off. In 2018, Northridge Hospital staff learned of her condition while Cox was hospitalized and alerted law enforcement. After a few attempts, the FBI, with the help of the Pilipino Workers Center, rescued Lugasan from Cox's townhome in Northridge, and she was eventually reunited with family. Cox pled guilty to a count of forced labor and was sentenced to house arrest and ordered to pay Lugasan restitution. In 2020, Lugasan passed away after contracting COVID-19 at her nursing home in Long Beach. (Courtesy of *Asian Journal*.)

Due to the San Fernando Valley's vast geography, unique political structure as part of the City of Los Angeles, and proximity to central Los Angeles, organizing the Filipino American community in the Valley is difficult, resulting in very few organized bodies. Most Filipino organizing centers around the church. Sirkulo, an organization comprised of Filipino immigrant parishioners of Our Lady of the Valley Church in Canoga Park, was formed in the 1980s for socialization. Above is the Sirkulo group operating a food booth at the parish's annual carnival during the early 1990s. Church groups with large Filipino congregations also organize traditional Christmas Simbang Gabi celebrations that bring communities together in the early morning. Below is the choir at St. Jane de Chantal Church in North Hollywood singing during a Simbang Gabi mass at 5:00 a.m. (Above, courtesy of the Araneta family; below, author's collection.)

Ferdinand Reyes has lived in Chatsworth for many years. Here, he is presiding over a meeting of Southern California Radio Pinoy, a short-lived radio station. (Courtesy of Max Reyes.)

The San Fernando Valley Filipino American Chamber of Commerce was formed in 2001 by community leaders Joe Arciaga, Rick Rolda, and Leo Maranan. As one of the few Filipino organizations representing the Valley, the chamber became an advocate for the region's Filipino businesses. The group has since evolved and rebranded to help businesses beyond the Valley. Pictured here are the chamber's leaders during the organization's early years. (Courtesy of Jomari Arciaga.)

Here are the members of the Balucas family in Sepulveda (now known as North Hills) in 1988. Pictured from left to right are Sami Linn Balucas, Gloria Ilejay Balucas, Sam Balucas, Lori Balucas Segrue, and Cheryl Balucas Church. Sam Balucas was one of the founders and longtime president of the Los Angeles chapter of the Filipino American National Historical Society (FANHS). (Courtesy of Shades of L.A. Photo Collection, Los Angeles Public Library.)

UPLIFT is an organization of undocumented Asian and Pacific Islander (undocuAPI) youth in Southern California, formed to develop immigrant rights leaders, build community, and uplift undocuAPI narratives. Many of its Filipino members live in the Valley. In 2014, an UPLIFT mother suggested that they celebrate Thanksgiving together, and it has since become an annual tradition. Here is the first UPLIFT "Friendsgiving" at the Villanueva Van Nuys home. (Courtesy of Madison Villanueva.)

On December 28, 1982, Reynaldo Banzali Estrada was tragically killed in a car accident at the intersection of Lindley Avenue and Vanowen Street while driving to deliver Christmas presents to relatives. His children luckily survived the accident but had to be saved from the vehicle by the jaws of life. Here is the life celebration of Estrada at St. Catherine of Siena Church on Sherman Way in Reseda. He was only 46 years old. (Both, courtesy of Marie and Reanne Estrada.)

On August 10, 1999, Buford Furrow Jr., a self-professed white supremacist, fatally shot Filipino American postal worker Joseph Santos Ileto in Chatsworth following a rampage where he fired 70 shots inside the North Valley Jewish Community Center. Ileto was delivering mail when Furrow approached and shot him nine times, later admitting to killing Ileto for being a federal employee and "looked Latino or Asian." Filipino communities across the country spoke out and condemned the racist act. Seen here is a march in honor of Ileto and victims of hate crimes. On the 20th anniversary of Joseph Ileto's murder, the US Postal Service commemorated his death with a plaque at the Chatsworth Post Office. After Ileto's murder, his family never stopped speaking out against hate and advocating for stronger hate crime and gun control laws. (Above, courtesy of AP Photo/Randi Lynn Beach; below, author's collection.)

Legendary farmworker organizer Philip Vera Cruz immigrated to the United States in 1926 and worked as a farmworker like many Filipinos during the era. In 1959, he founded the Agricultural Workers Organizing Committee (AWOC). Along with other Filipino and Mexican labor leaders, Vera Cruz was instrumental in leading the 1965 Delano Grape Strike, the largest successful agricultural strike in history. He also helped form the Farm Workers Credit Union and create Agbayani Village, a retirement community for older farmworkers. Observant and aware of the individual egos that afflict leaders and often derail larger movements, Vera Cruz once wrote, "Leadership is only incidental to the movement. It is the movement that is the most important thing." Pictured is Vera Cruz at the age of 91 speaking at Cal State Northridge about the importance of workers' rights and interethnic solidarity. (Courtesy of Moonie Lantion.)

With a long history of Filipinos in the medical industry from American colonization, many Filipino immigrants found an employment niche in the American economy as caregivers for elderly Americans. Likewise, many Filipino Americans found an entrepreneurial niche in owning and running care homes for the elderly and other assisted living facilities. Across the Valley, Filipinos live and work in many of these unassuming facilities, somewhat obscuring their important presence in the suburban landscape. Seen here are employees of the now-closed Porter Ranch Summer Home in Northridge during the 1990s. (Both, courtesy of the Bernardo family.)

In some cases, caregivers are exploited because care work is largely unregulated. Through the organizing of the Pilipino Workers Center, Adat Shalom, who operated six facilities in the Valley, was ordered to pay $8.4 million in lost wages and damages to former employees—mostly immigrant Filipinas. Pictured is a 2022 demonstration at Adat Shalom's West Hills location with organizer Lolita Lledo leading the chants. (Courtesy of the Pilipino Workers Center.)

The Kaiser Permanente Hospital in Panorama City attracts many Filipinos searching for employment, which was among the reasons why Filipinos settled in the area. Working for Kaiser, however, was never completely harmonious, particularly during the COVID-19 pandemic, when Filipino front liners died at an alarmingly higher rate than other workers. Fighting for better working conditions and proper staffing, hospital workers protest at the hospital in 2023. (Courtesy of AP Photo/Richard Vogel.)

During the 1990s, California college campuses became hotbeds of debate over affirmative action as conservative forces sought to end race-based policies in public education. The passage of Proposition 209 in 1996 eventually dealt a blow to affirmative action, prohibiting state governmental institutions from considering race, sex, or ethnicity in public employment, public contracting, and public education. Nonetheless, many Filipino American youths across California were adamant in stopping anti–affirmative action legislation. Seen here from left to right are Allan Aquino, Lisa Casabar Ulanday, Louie Ulanday, and Jeremiah Martin at a pro–affirmative action rally on the campus of Cal State Northridge in 1995. Below are Carlo Medina, Cheryl Atienza, Mark Macalintal, and Alex Reyes performing the dance Tinikling in front of the Oviatt Library during a 1996 rally organized by the Coalition for Affirmative Action, which featured civil rights leader Jesse Jackson. (Both, courtesy of Moonie Lantion.)

On January 22, 2024, the California Faculty Association (CFA) launched a strike at all 23 campuses of the California State University system, calling for equitable compensation, just benefits, and better working conditions. It was the largest strike in the history of American higher education. On this rainy day in Southern California, hundreds of Cal State Northridge faculty, staff, students, and supporters, including Asian American studies professor Tracy Lachica Buenavista (below), led demonstrations just outside of campus. (Both, courtesy of Tracy Lachica Buenavista.)

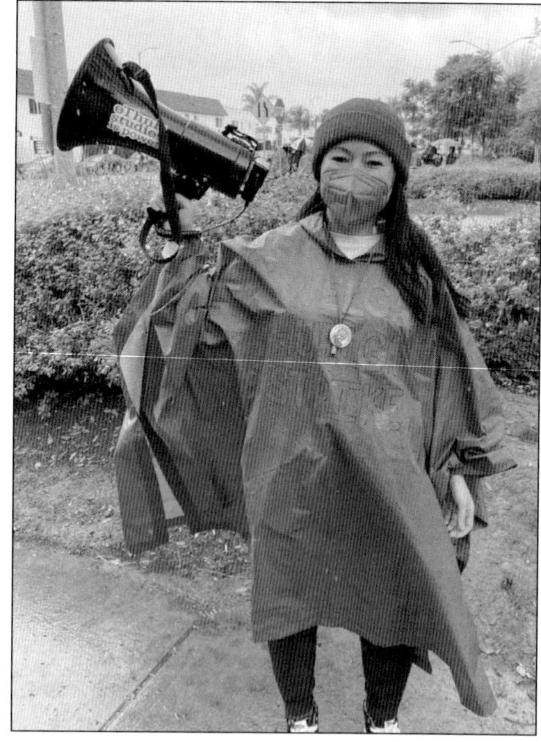

Marvin and Pierre Mercado began the notorious gang Asian Boyz from their Van Nuys apartment in the early 1990s. In 1995, the gang went on a crime spree, dubbed the "Summer of Madness," which included eight murders. After several arrests, the Mercados fled to the Philippines until they were found in 2007 and then later sentenced to life imprisonment. Here is Marvin Mercado during his sentence hearing. (Courtesy of AP Photo/Nick Ut.)

At the height of gang hysteria in Southern California, some school administrators targeted Filipino youth for possible gang affiliation. At Bishop Alemany High School, school officials expelled eight students and suspended four students in 1996 over their association with a group called II Romantik. School parents protested this decision, saying it was a severe overreaction and racially motivated. Here are the students with supposed gang ties. (Courtesy of Berto Ponce.)

Pictured are Rhonda Munar and her mother, Leonora Munar, placing a 50-pound bag of rice into their cart at the Burbank Costco. In 2008, amid a global crisis where shortages caused a sharp increase in rice prices, many Filipinos stocked up their supply. As one of the highest consumers of rice, Filipinos depend on the grain as the most integral part of their diets. (Courtesy of AP Photo/Damian Dovarganes.)

The Kingdom of Jesus Christ Church is a Philippine-based church founded and led by Apollo Quiboloy, the self-proclaimed "Appointed Son of God." Notorious for a lavish lifestyle, Quiboloy had an extravagant home in Calabasas. In 2020, the FBI charged him and other church officials with sex trafficking, fraud, and coercion. Here is the Kingdom of Jesus Christ US headquarters in Van Nuys following the charges. (Courtesy of AP Photo/Richard Vogel.)

On May 13, 2022, Nerissa Roque and her daughter Patricia were at a McDonald's drive-thru in North Hollywood when a drunk white man named Nicholas Weber yelled racist slurs and threatened to kill them. When Gabriel Roque, Patricia's father, arrived, Weber attacked him, causing a broken rib, then tried to choke Nerissa. The incident occurred during the anti-Asian hate escalation from the COVID-19 pandemic, and the family insisted the assault was a hate crime. After a year of hearings and delays, which included the judge dropping hate crime enhancements due to a technicality, Weber was given a plea deal. The incident nevertheless galvanized Filipino Americans to fight for justice. Above is the Roque family at a rally outside the Van Nuys courthouse, and below is the newly formed Anakbayan San Fernando Valley at another rally. (Both, courtesy of Anakbayan San Fernando Valley.)

Panorama Senior High School, a public school in the Los Angeles Unified School District, opened its doors in 2006 and serves the Panorama City, Arleta, and Van Nuys neighborhoods. On the site of a former Carnation testing facility, the high school serves over 1,000 students, including a significant number of Filipino Americans. This is a group photograph of the school's Filipino Club and future community leaders of the San Fernando Valley in the classroom of math teacher and club advisor Josefina Palma. (Author's collection.)

Bibliography

Allen, James A., and Eugene Turner. *The Ethnic Quilt: Population Diversity in Southern California.* Northridge: Center for Geographical Studies, California State University, Northridge, 1997.

Asian Journal.

Barraclough, Laura R. *Making the San Fernando Valley: Rural Landscapes, Urban Development, and White Privilege.* Athens: University of Georgia Press, 2011.

Bernardo, Joseph. "From 'Little Brown Brothers' to 'Forgotten Asian Americans': Race, Space, and Empire in Filipino Los Angeles." PhD diss., University of Washington, 2014.

De Guzman, Jean Paul. "And Make the San Fernando Valley My Home: Contested Spaces, Identities, and Activism on the Edge of Los Angeles." PhD diss., University of California, Los Angeles, 2014.

Hise, Greg. *Magnetic Los Angeles: Planning the Twentieth Century Metropolis.* Baltimore: Johns Hopkins University Press, 1997.

Los Angeles Times.

Meet the 818.

Nicolaides, Becky. *The New Suburbia: How Diversity Remade Suburban Life in Los Angeles after 1945.* Oxford: Oxford University Press, 2024.

Roderick, Kevin. *The San Fernando Valley: America's Suburb.* Los Angeles: Los Angeles Times Books, 2001.

Shoutout LA.

Tongson, Karen. *Relocations: Queer Suburban Imaginaries.* New York: New York University Press, 2011.

Voyage LA Magazine.

Zarsadiaz, James. *Resisting Change in Suburbia: Asian Immigrants and Frontier Nostalgia in L.A.* Berkeley: University of California Press, 2022.

Consistent with our mission to preserve history on a local level, this book was printed in South Carolina on American-made paper and manufactured entirely in the United States. Products carrying the accredited Forest Stewardship Council (FSC) label are printed on 100 percent FSC-certified paper.